Bait Angling for Common Fishes

"Izaak Walton teaching his scholar how to land a fish—"

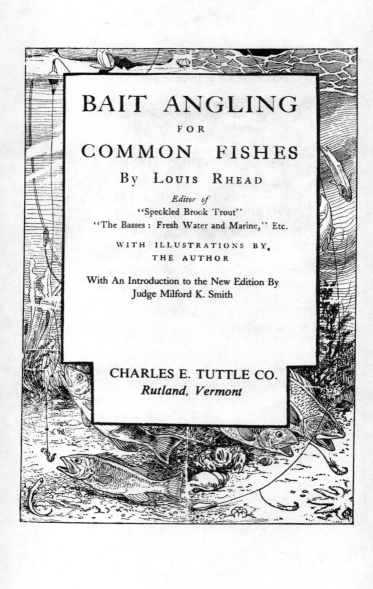

BAIT ANGLING

FOR

COMMON FISHES

By Louis Rhead

Editor of
"Speckled Brook Trout"
"The Basses : Fresh Water and Marine," Etc.

WITH ILLUSTRATIONS BY
THE AUTHOR

With An Introduction to the New Edition By
Judge Milford K. Smith

CHARLES E. TUTTLE CO.
Rutland, Vermont

REPRESENTATIVES
For Continental Europe:
BOXERBOOKS, INC., Zurich

For the British Isles:
PRENTICE-HALL INTERNATIONAL,
INC., London

For Canada
HURTIG PUBLISHERS, Edmonton

For Australasia:
PAUL FLESCH & CO., PTY. LTD.
C/O BOOKWISE AUSTRALIA
104 Sussex Street, Sydney

Published by the Charles E. Tuttle Company, Inc.
of Rutland, Vermont

Library of Congress Catalog Card No. 75-28715
International Standard Book No. 0-8048-1168-7

First edition published 1907
by Outing Publishing Company, New York
First Tuttle edition published 1975

Printed in USA

INTRODUCTION
TO NEW EDITION

Louis Rhead was one of the foremost angling writers in the early part of this century. His books, beautifully illustrated by the author were gospel to an earlier generation of anglers. His drawings of various fishes actually on the point of engulfing an offered bait, aroused the fishing fever in a whole generation of beginning fishermen.

Rhead was aware that bait fishing was an art in itself, and although he was also an accomplished angler with the fly, his "Bait Angling For Common Fishes", still remains a classic on this most natural method for fishing for the finny inhabitants of stream, lake and ocean. Louis Rhead knew that it was bait fishing that introduced the boy to the joys of fishing. He was also aware that older men enjoyed the primitive method of pole, line, hook and bait, to furnish sport for themselves and food for their families. What was true in his day, is also true today.

Louis Rhead, while detailing the best bait fishing methods for such game species as brook trout and walleyed pike, knew that to many fishermen such common species as sunfish, perch, bullheads and even eels furnished fair sport and good eating. He has the insight to know that to the young fisherman, fish are fish, and all are desirable. He recognized that there would be those who read his book who fished the salty ocean waters as well as the fresh water streams and lakes, and he instructs his readers on the proper way to bait fish for the more common salt water fish.

"Bait Angling For Common Fishes" is a book that was written for less sophisticated times, and with less sophisticated fishing tackle than is today available. But fishes and their appetites have not varied since Rhead wrote his book, and the methods and baits he describes will take fish as readily today as they did yesterday.

The older angler will find this book a collector's item, bringing to mind again the days when catching a fish of any kind was a minor miracle, and recapturing the rapture of his early fishing days. It should have an honored place in any well rounded angling library.

The young angler, just starting his fishing career, or the man who is just a once in a while fisherman, and whose main desire is to bring home enough fish for a dinner, "Bait Angling For Common Fishes" is a basic primer for fishing. Surprisingly, while the book stores are well stocked with volumes on the more or less esoteric arts of fly fishing, a few books have appeared on the simpler sport of bait fishing, since Rhead's day.

There are few angling books that can arouse the nostalgia of the older angler, and provide the means of entering successfully the brotherhood of the angler for the young fisherman. "Bait Angling For Common Fishes" is one of this rare lot. Charles E. Tuttle Co., Inc. deserves the gratitude of all fishermen for its reprint of this fishing classic.

Milford K. Smith.

CONTENTS

ILLUSTRATIONS

PREFACE

THE purpose of this volume is to be a handy guide of practical information on how to angle for common and familiar bottom fishes, and descriptions of their habits for amateurs and young people who have not the opportunity or the means to wander afar in search of game fish, which some consider more worthy. Certainly our common fishes are more accessible, as well as more plentiful, and are in most cases bottom feeders. Many men, especially with a family, prefer to spend their holidays and vacations in the mountains or on the seashore, and, though not anglers, often share in the innocent primitive methods of pole, string and pin-hook. The writer does not here claim the eel to be more gamey than the bass, but he shows a proper method whereby more real enjoyment is to be had in bottom fishing than that now commonly practiced. In England bottom or "coarse fishing" (as they term it)

Preface

has received considerable attention, many important works have been written, but in America numberless volumes on salmon, trout and other game fish have appeared, but I am not aware of any that have been written on angling for the commoner and more familiar fishes, such as may be found in this work.

There are many women who like to fish, but dislike to put a worm on and take a fish off the hook. This difficulty is soon overcome, if she explains to any boy, who will invariably place his services at her disposal, and loudly applaud her luck.

The trout is not a bottom fish, but I have included it because at times it is fished for in that way.

For the methods of fishing I have added to my own that practiced by other anglers, and for the descriptive habits I am indebted to the works of Brown Goode, Scott, Harris, and mostly to " The Food and Game Fish of New York," by my friend, Tarleton H. Bean.

Bait Angling for Common Fishes

THE WORM AS A BAIT

FISHING with a worm is not held in such high estimation as it deserves, a circumstance entirely owing to its being but very imperfectly understood. Flyfishers are apt to sneer at worm fishing as a thing so simple that any one may succeed in it, yet a live worm is the most effective, deadly all-round bait available; for all the fishes that swim, either in fresh or in salt water, from the plebeian and lowly catfish to the lordly salmon, at all seasons, daytime or nighttime, it is resistless and bound to be seized with avidity, especially if properly impaled on a hook which is of the right size. Nature's bountiful provision of an inexhaustible supply makes the worm a poor man's friend; no matter where he digs in suitable soil, a few minutes will suffice to amply supply him with all that is needed to capture and provide a mess of fish for himself and his family. With the aid of a small hook and some fine line, the combined expense of but a few cents, his outfit used with care and judgment, he is as successful as the rich man with expensive tackle and fly-book. Of course, the highest art in worm fishing is that practiced by salmon and trout anglers, not the ever-present worm plugger of mountain brooks, but the expert who captures the wary trout in low and clear water during June and July. One advantage it possesses over the fly is the superior size of the trout caught. It is just as important that the bait be prepared properly, in that the angler may succeed in landing more fish of larger size; the worm, then, requires some preparation as well as due care in placing it before the quarry. In using worms for chub, dace, perch, wall eye, and sunfish there is a great advantage in having them well scoured and of proper size. There are four kinds of worms most esteemed by anglers. The black-headed worm, found in good garden soil, is free from the knot which most worms have, and is rather dark in color; it is the most durable of all worms. Then there is the brantling, found in old dung hills or similar places. It may be known by being ringed all round with a knot a little above the middle, and it is somewhat flat. One objection to it is its extreme softness; it is incapable of being toughened. The marsh worm when taken from the earth is of a pale blue color with a whitish knot a little above the center. It is a very small worm, and when kept long enough becomes a lively pink color and most killing for dace, sunfish and chub. It is the most plentiful, and may be found in any garden among heaps of decayed leaves or rubbish and below stones. The red-headed worm is only found plentifully in the very richest soil about the edge of dung

3

hills. It is thick in proportion to its length, and a dark red color down the back, pale blue underneath. It is not so good as those before mentioned, for the reason that it soon loses its color after being a short time in the water; it is best suited for perch, wall-eye and eels. A small bright, clean worm is always more enticing than a large thick worm. It is a great error to suppose that a large worm insures the capture of large sized fish, it is quite the reverse, as a large worm will seldom capture anything but some audacious little fellow. When worms are newly dug, they are so full of earth as to be unfit for use. Brantlings may be scoured in a day or two, but the other kinds require to be kept at least a week. Immediately on being dug they should be well washed in clear water, and placed in an earthenware jar with plenty of moss. The moss should be well washed and wrung as hard as possible, and all the sticks and straws picked out, as they are apt to cut the worms. The jar should be examined every second or third day, and all the dead or sickly worms removed, the moss changed and a few small pieces of bread and a spoonful of milk put on the moss for their nourishment. The process of toughening worms can only be accomplished by keeping the moss dry, so that the worms may lose some of the moisture of their bodies and thus become tough and more durable. Of course, if carried to any great extent it impairs their vitality, which gives them a withered look. When thoroughly divested of earthy matter, worms can be easily baited, and will last quite long alive for the purpose needed. It is important that the worm jar should be kept always in a cool place. For eels and catfish, there is no need to use scoured worms; but for chub, dace, trout, wall-eye, sunfish, perch, the two latter, especially, it is of great value, and it is also well to choose the right kind of worm, the red-headed worm is best for perch and wall-eye, the brantling is better for chub, dace and sunfish.

When impaling the worm on the hook, it is not necessary to pierce the hook through the middle of the body, but it can be, and is quite sufficient to hook it just through the skin; it will hold if the barb is sharp. In that way it enables the worm to act much more lively while in the water; it is the lively kicking movement that most attracts the fish. A dead worm is of no value to tempt a fish to take it. Be careful to remove little bits of white remnants of previous worms: they should never be left on the hook.

Regarding the sand and bloodworms for salt water fishing, no scouring is needed, but they should be kept at no higher temperature than their natural element of mud or sand. They are kept longer in sea plants or weeds just kept damp and cool, the seaweed containing sufficient salt to retain their freshness.

Many anglers put the hook right through the middle of the body, and so let out all the blood, which of course takes life

6

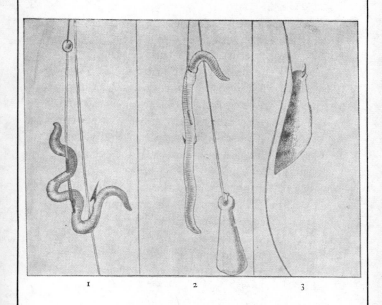

1 Single hooked worm
2 Double hooked worm
3 Cut fish-tail spinner

Proper Method of Hooking Bait

away with it, and all that remains is a white piece of tape on the hook, not near so attractive as the natural wriggling worm. Any fish whose mouth is large enough to take a bloodworm takes the hook right in its mouth, so that it is much better if the worm is hooked by the skin, first at one end, then in the middle, also at the other end; by this means the worm lives, acts in a natural manner more attractive to the fish, drawing them to the bait much sooner, and entices them to take it with greater avidity. Blood and sandworms are quite long enough to allow at least an inch of each end to hang down and so wriggle. There is one disadvantage in hooking by the skin in the fact that smaller kinds than those fished for are apt to more easily tear the bait off and get away with it, but I find this happens less often than might be supposed, for the larger fish drive small ones away when they see a kicking worm.

7

THE CATFISH OR BULLHEAD

THE right name of this popular and well-known fish is the horned pout, and is of a wide distribution, being found in ponds, lakes and streams all over the United States and Canada. It multiplies so rapidly in any kind of water that it soon clears all edible matter which would be useful food for better fish. This species reaches a maximum length of eighteen inches and a weight of four pounds, but the average size of market specimens is much smaller. There are many species of this family, each rejoicing in a number of names, the largest kind being the lake catfish, sometimes caught in the Mississippi River weighing over a hundred pounds. In Lake Erie specimens have been taken up to fifty pounds. The United States Bureau of Fisheries propagate and distribute the most valuable members of the family, the channel catfish, spotted cat, yellow cat, black cat, marbled cat, blue cat, black bullhead and the pout.

They are all dull, slow-moving fish, but when hooked are surprisingly lively; all are fond of mud, growing best in weedy ponds and rivers without a current. They stay near the bottom, moving slowly about, with their barbels widely spread, watching for anything eatable. The catfishes are a hardy race, and are very tenacious of life, opening and shutting their mouths half an hour after their heads have been cut off, and so prolific are they that in some places the bottom of the water seems a living mass of fish. At such times, through lack of food, they die in thousands, never attaining a size of more than six inches. Living entirely at the bottom armed with long sharp spines, they are comparatively safe from enemies and at the end of the third year are fully matured. Spawning in spring, when the young are hatched, the old fish lead them in great schools near the shore, seemingly caring for them as a hen does her chicks. The very young fish look like little black tadpoles, and the spines are strongly developed at an early age. The old fish accompanies the brood for a certain time, always swimming around the swarm of young in order to keep them together. When alarmed, the parent dashes off, the whole swarm following on. When the mature fish grow to a large size they feed on the young of their own species if their food is scarce. Many instances are recorded where a small fish having been hooked, a larger fish has taken and swallowed it, and so got caught. Although considered the poor man's food, the catfish, if properly prepared and cooked, makes an excellent pan fish, enjoyed by all classes of people. Its flesh is white and juicy, the main objection to it being mostly on account of its repulsive appearance, and for this reason when they are sent to market the head is cut off and the body skinned.

The catfish retains its freshness much

longer than any other fish, and it has comparatively few bones. The demand for it as a market fish is growing to such an extent that there have arisen extensive and almost special fisheries for it in the south, the Mississippi Valley, and region of the Great Lakes, which is the center of their greatest abundance. In late years however, the demand for these fish has reached such dimensions that in some localities such extensive inroads have been made upon their numbers that it has become a problem how to restock the depleted waters. It is only in the last few years that it has been considered necessary to resort to the artificial propagation of catfishes. Dr. Tarleton Bean has much to say in favor of this fish. Brown Goode says: "If taken from clear cold water it is very palatable, when properly cooked, even delicious; in texture and flavor resembling the eel." Opinions seem to be about evenly divided as to the worth of this fish. Some writers consider it the most unattractive fish of our fresh waters, and to catch it represents the lowest depths of depravity in fishing with hook and line. This of course depends on the manner and method of fishing. Dr. Bean tells in his "Food and Game Fish" that in Lake Erie catfish are taken chiefly by means of set lines, and the fishing is best during June, July and August. The method consists of from two hundred to four hundred hooks attached by short lines to a main line, which is from five to seven fathoms long, according to the place in which set, the line being held in place by poles or stakes pushed into the mud. Herring or grasshoppers are used for bait, and the fish taken average eight or ten pounds' weight. Some of the lines have as many as two thousand hooks.

The catfish is a ready and voracious feeder, any kind of bait being greedily swallowed, and a large fish, when he feels the hook, goes for some distance at astonishing speed, pulling and tugging with bull-like strength. In angling for them with rod and line the worm is perhaps the best and most convenient bait. They will take with nearly the same avidity minnows, grasshoppers, small frogs, a piece of salt mackerel, or pork, as well as pieces of fresh fish cut from the under part of a chub, sunfish or perch, that part which has the fin attached. As the catfish always gorges the bait, his mouth being large and capacious, the hook is extracted much easier if it is a good size; No. 5 or No. 6 Limerick hooks will do. If the young angler does not possess a split bamboo, a light rod of native cane ten feet long will be of ample service. The line should be of twisted silk, the same length as the rod and tied to the tip, doing away with the use of the reel.

As to a leader, it is unnecessary, but a three-foot leader, like the one used for perch, makes the outfit seem more like game fishing, and the leader is useful because it stands up better from the bait than when snells only are in use. I have seen catfish caught without even snells, the hook being merely tied to the line. If the bait is too light to sink quickly, two or three split shot can be attached to the line so that it will rapidly drop to the bottom, one shot on the snell, the other six inches above. In bottom fishing a float is always an advantage; it keeps the line from floating toward the angler, and it also enables him to cast more deftly among and around weeds. It can be adjusted according to the depth of the water, which can be tested by a weighted sinker, so that the float stands up and the bait lies on the bottom. This proper adjustment of float and bait is most important, for the reason that when the bait is taken quicker action is acquired. Two hooks can be tied, one a foot above the other, with a different kind of bait on each. The piece of pork or dead fish is better placed on the bottom hook, and the live wriggling worm above. If the catfish are plentiful it will be but a short time before the float shows signs that something is going on, and in a minute or so the float goes under and the fish is on. If it is a large fish let him run. Immediately he stops it is time to work the cat toward the surface. He is sure to be fast, so that there need be no hurry in landing him. When he is pulled ashore or in the boat the greatest care should be taken in handling him, as the horns on his fins make nasty wounds. The hook will be far down his throat, and the best way to extract it is to have a sharp knife with which to slit open his stomach to the gills; if the head is severed the hook will be cut from the snell and become useless for further fishing. If the fish is a large one of three or four pounds, the foot should be placed on the middle of his back, holding tight on the line, then placing the knife through the gills cut the under side. In running streams the catfish is more gamey and will often make strong rushes, swimming behind a large stone, and then crawl under, so that some time will elapse before he can be dislodged.

It often happens that in fishing such

streams a trout or bass will take the worm and play quite a different game, so that it is always wise to have tackle equal to such an emergency. In such cases it is well to be slow and careful; instead of lifting such fish bodily from the water lead it gently toward the bank of the stream and run it up over the stones or sand. Catfish do not congregate in shallow water, they prefer to lie in deep holes in the mud or sand, most often near weeds and vegetable matter. There is no special time of day to fish, any time will do, day or night, and the best season to catch them is the warm months of July and August. In small rivers and ponds large numbers are caught by the country people solely for edible purposes, by placing set lines over night with twenty to fifty hooks on a line placed across the stream. The next morning the line is pulled up and nearly every hook has been taken. These lines are nearly always baited with worms or small pieces of liver. After a fair-sized mess has been caught it is best to prepare them at once while they are fresh. To properly skin them, the head should be cut from below, leaving the skin attached to the shoulders. By placing a small pinch of salt on the fingers a tighter grip on the skin will enable it to be easily pulled from the body. The fish can then be cleaned and afterward placed in salt and water; more salt is needed if the fish have been taken from quiet, stagnant water. The salt takes away the muddy taste, so noticeable in nearly all bottom-feeding fish. After being immersed in salt water a few hours, they can be sharply and quickly fried in hot fat. If the epicure tries them without knowing what fish they are, it is very certain he will pronounce catfish a tasty and nutritious dish. Dr. Bean mentions a dish of catfish caught in Chautauqua Lake that he enjoyed quite as much as trout, though much depends, of course on how they are cooked. If cooked without being skinned they are quite disagreeable and of a very unpleasant odor.

17

THE EEL

THE common eel is another bottom fish that is caught extensively by hand lines, mostly at evening or nighttime, for the reason that it is nocturnal in its habits, sleeping or lying in the mud with its head just peeping out during the day. It dislikes sunny spots, and prefers to lie in the shadow of piles and bridges. It is a most voracious feeder, devouring great quantities of the fry of other fishes, being one of the greatest enemies of the spawn of trout and other game fish. On their food-hunting excursions they turn over huge and small stones alike, working for hours if necessary, beneath which they find species of shrimp and crayfish, of which they are particularly fond. Nothing in the shape of living thing comes amiss to an eel, aquatic insects, water beetles, everything that lives in the water it will prey upon. They are among the most powerful and rapid of swimmers, and on light tackle give good accounts of their strength. Eels have been known to grow to a length of four feet, but the average is about two feet. They breed in salt water; both adults and the young ascend the streams from the sea sometimes a distance of five hundred miles. The young have been seen in countless millions making their way up to fresh water. It is known that, while on their way, if the large ones meet obstructions in streams, they will leave the water and travel through wet grass at night, or over moist rocks, until they arrive at some water that is suited to their mode of living. They delight to lie, buried in the mud or sand, with only their heads out, waiting and ready to pounce on any-thing edible that comes within their reach. They are also often found in the long grass of shallow-running clear streams. In such conditions they are not only more agree-able to eat, but more difficult to catch.

In such water they are speared at night-time, when the spearer wades down, and with the aid of a lantern, sees them swimming about. The best way to angle for eels is to drop the bait in some sandy or muddy bottom; always near long grass or weeds. Use a strong, light rod without the reel, and have the line tied at the tip; or, if the angler wishes to play him, with the reel in the usual way, much more sport is the result, though an eel often runs under a rock, and no amount of tugging will loosen him, so that both the line and gut leader should be stout and strong. A float may be attached to the line to keep the bait out of the weeds and give the angler more free play with the line. Use No. 7 or No. 8 hooks baited with a small red worm, which should be allowed to drag and lie at the bottom. The worm as a bait for eels is the most deadly, as it is with all bottom feeders. While the eel will take almost anything in the shape of food, worms are exceedingly attractive, even more so than live minnows; this applies to both pond as well as river fishing.

The eel requires considerable indulgence when he takes the bait, and as soon as he is pulled out of the water, whether big or little, the angler should stamp his foot across his body, holding the line tight with one hand and with the other cut through his gills with a sharp knife, taking care of course not to cut the gut, which is almost always some distance down his throat. This is the quickest and most humane method to prevent the slippery rascal from tying the line full of knots and twisting it inextricably round his body, very often breaking the line and so getting away. In fact he is so lively on being taken from the water that more often he gets away than is captured. For that reason the eel is not a fish suited to women anglers, as the extraordinary contortions could hardly be managed by them. With boys, the case differs, for they enjoy the excitement and difficulty of unhooking the wriggling terror, which becomes infinitely more troublesome when fishing after dark. Good eel fishing is best in dams and near mill wheels. Sitting on the bank by the waterside at evening, properly prepared with bait and tackle, also a small lantern, this fish provides quite a diversion. Eel fishing in salt water is also very popular when it is done from a boat, which should be anchored near the edge of channels, on soft or sandy or muddy bottoms. The rod is seldom brought into play for sea fishing, simply a stout line with a strong leader and a heavy sinker to keep the bait on the bottom. If the sinker is not heavy enough to withstand the tide and keep to the bottom, more weight should be added. Eels will not rise from the bottom for food. The hook should be attached close to the sinker, and two or three hooks may be used, and should be No. 8 to No. 10 Sproat. By far the best bait in salt water is the shedder crab, but sandworms, killies, clams or even pieces of fish will take them. Many anglers use a

long-shanked hook, which is more convenient to hold the fish from wriggling,
and more important still, enables the fish
to be taken from the hook much easier.
When the fish bites strike hard, and if
hooked, lose no time in bringing him up
over the side of the boat. After it is in the
boat, before taking out the hook, get a
good tight grip on the body with the help
of the line, then slap the tail smartly on
the edge of the boat, which stuns the fish,
for the tail is very sensitive, and by this
means time is saved in getting the hook
free.

Another species of sea eel is that called
the conger eel, and which occasionally is
caught by hand lines. It sometimes grows
to thirty pounds' weight. In England this
same fish is often caught up to seventy
pounds. Sea fishermen dislike to handle
the conger on account of its great pug-
nacity as well as strength. It is a savage
brute, with long jaws lined with long sharp
teeth, and it snaps viciously at everything

near it when captured, and the only sure way out of the difficulty is to rap it hard on the top of the skull with a stout stick or knotted rope. The conger is not numerous; few are caught, and they are landed mostly when angling for other fish with large pieces of clams or cut fish. The conger eel is extremely good eating, with white flaky flesh; though rather soft it has a peculiar taste, rather sweet, I think, but very different from cod or halibut. The common eel is perhaps the most palatable of all bottom fishes; when caught in running clear water no fish is equal to it, if well cooked; the flavor is sweet and the flesh nutritious, especially if stewed and served with a sauce of parsley butter. The popular mode of cooking eels is, however, by frying them in plenty of fat or good olive oil. A large number of eels are pickled and salted, but whatever way they are prepared each of them makes a savory dish.

Carp

Catfish

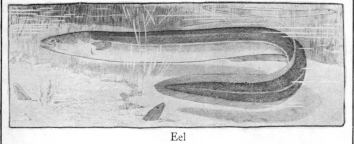

Eel

THE PERCH

YELLOW perch, also known as ring perch, striped perch and raccoon perch, are among the most strikingly marked and best known fresh-water fishes. They are found from Nova Scotia to North Carolina in coast-wise waters, and are very abundant in large ponds, lakes and many of the streams.

It is a certain fact that more people, including amateurs, women and young folks angle for perch than any other fresh-water fish. The reason is not far to seek. They are ready biters, strong and voracious feeders, and can be caught on any bait—small minnows, worms, crickets, grasshoppers, small frogs, crawfish and small spoons. They will rise to an artificial fly, and will ravenously take one of the brightly colored fins of their own species, if placed on a hook and skittered quickly over the surface.

25

Bait Angling for Common Fishes

Perch frequent quiet waters of moderate depth, pools under hollow banks, eddies and shady reaches in the meadow brooks, creeks and canals, preferring the sides of the streams to swift currents, and sandy and pebbly rather than muddy bottoms. In mill ponds they are likely to be found in deep waters just above the dam, and in the vicinity of piles of locks, bridges and sluice gates. They sometimes descend into brackish water of estuaries, where they become large and very firm fleshed. In muddy pools they often assume a golden color, but in such situations are soft of flesh and not well flavored. They love to be among long weeds, grasses and lily pads in large lakes, and seem to thrive in neighborly friendship with the bass, pike and pickerel—their strong array of sharp spines probably protects them from those savage and predaceous fish. The largest specimens are found in rivers, where the bed of the water is partially covered with vegetation in a slow-moving current.

The Perch

They are gregarious, always in schools, and the fish of a school will be about of a uniform size, be that great or small. When the young angler meets a school of good-sized perch, he may capture every one, if he be noiseless and wary. The usual length of the yellow perch is less than ten inches, and its average weight less than a pound, though specimens have been caught up to four pounds. In feeding, they chase small minnows instead of waiting for a single fish to come near enough to seize by a single dart upon it, as the pickerel does. They are not rapid in their movements, but seem to dart with open mouth at several minnows, as though to catch some of the number they pursue.

Many of the old writers treat of the perch with contempt—Forrester, Scott, Norris and Robert B. Roosevelt, all have a fling at this hardy and gamey fish. Mr. Roosevelt in his book on game fishes in a spirit of levity says: " Their flesh is coarse, white and tasteless, and they are pursued only by boys and ladies." On the other hand Seth Green admits that " it is an excellent fish for the people who have neither time, money nor patience for long trips and complicated tackle," and also pronounces it " a superior table fish, and if taken on a light rod and tackle with an artificial fly, it affords not a little sport."

The simplest way to catch perch is with the boys' standard outfit, a pole, a stout line, large float and a heavy sinker, with a worm or minnow for bait. This, however, is effective only when the water is muddy, and the perch numerous and hungry. For wary large fish in clearer water more delicate tackle is necessary. The line should be fine, of enameled silk, a fly rod of six ounces, a light click reel and a small three-foot leader with two flies on No. 7 hooks. Then the yellow perch will not disappoint the most exacting angler who has a true love for the sport; under such circumstances it is a good gamey little fish, eager to rise, bold to a degree, and fights to a finish.

The Perch

For worm or minnow fishing, the float should be small and well balanced, and the shot for sinkers only heavy enough to keep the float steady. The float should be adjusted so that the bait may be suspended about a foot from the bottom, and a gentle motion upward and downward may be advantageously employed. No. 5 or No. 6 hooks on gut snell with a small swivel to connect the snell to the line may be used. For worm fishing from the boat landing or an anchored boat in eight or ten feet of gently running water, there are two ways to fish. The first is to place the sinker on the line so that the bait will touch the bottom; in that case the worm should always be lively and kicking, the hook well covered, with only one worm—a large bunch of half a dozen worms is unnatural. Another way is to have the bait two feet from the bottom, so that the running water will drift it back and forth; it is well to keep moving the float a foot or so, but in a gentle manner.

This method also applies to grasshoppers and crickets, which should be put on a No. 5 to No. 3 snell hook; grasshoppers should be hooked through the shoulders—both they and crickets will live for some time if hooked in the right way. In using a small minnow, hook him through both lips, near the tip of the nose, and on snelled hooks No. 1 to No. 3. The minnow, if put on alive will swim around till seen by the perch, and it should be placed so that it swims one or two feet from the bottom. When the fish strikes take plenty of time, so that the perch can properly gorge the fish. All fish take the minnow sideways first, then turn it around and swallow it head first, afterward move away—that is the time to strike and hook them. It should be done with a sharp, quick turn of the wrist, not a savage pull or long jerk. If the fish is a large one and he wants to play or fight, give him every chance. Perch make two or three runs, swiftly at times, come right up to the surface, then down again, but this happens mostly in running streams; in sluggish water they fight less, but kick more. Trolling or casting with a small single-hook spoon, or a live minnow without a spoon, will invariably capture large perch, in lakes or ponds. The boat should be rowed along slowly, not far from the shore and inside the weeds, or nearest the center of the lake, and as close to the weeds as possible without getting entangled. When the fish strikes, give him time, but hold the rod firm and steady, he will hook himself secure. The only thing the young angler has to do is to keep a taut line, then slowly reel in and boat him. In fishing for perch the angler cannot be too careful in unhooking these spike-armed heroes, for the armature of fins inflicts wounds painful and difficult to heal. In fly fishing for perch the best time is when the water is gently rippled by the wind, or from sundown to dusk, and in casting it is well to let the fly sink about a foot and work it about sharply through the water. Any trout or bass fly tied on a No. 5 to No. 3

hook is effective. I have caught perch on the brown palmer, coachman and silver doctor.

In England and France they have a method of fishing for perch not practiced here. It is called " pater-nostering," which simply consists in the use of a line of gut about four or five feet long, at the end of which is a sinker to keep it on the bottom; about six or eight inches above this is fastened a hook on some six inches of gut, a foot above this another hook is fixed on, and a foot above that again a third. This third hook is often a gimp hook, where pickerel and perch are found in common, so that if the pickerel should come to the bait there may be a fair chance of capturing him. A minnow being hooked through the lips on each of the other hooks, the tackle is dropped in an eddy where perch are supposed to be, and the three baits swim round and round the main line, so that no matter whether the fish are resting at the bottom or reaching for their prey in midwater, they may be attracted. As soon as there is a bite from a perch the angler feels it at the rod point, slackens line for two seconds to let the fish get the minnow well into his mouth, and then strikes. Should not a bite occur, the tackle is cast to a distance, and after being allowed to rest for a minute it is drawn in a few feet, when another cast is made, and then another draw, till the tackle is worked up to the boat or on the bank. This method has some advantages in the fact that it is possible to catch more fish. Sometimes two and even three are caught at once.

In the fall, perch become more wary; the large ones especially are so timid that if they see the angler they refuse to take the bait. Many fish are taken by fishing through the ice on the northern lakes, as the fish retire to deep water with a bottom of fine grass as the cold weather approaches. There they may be found in February and March, which is the time for ice fishing. The tools required are an ice chisel for cutting the holes, a hand line and sinker, fixed with a " spreader " and snells, and although it does not come under the head of tools, a fire. The spreader is a piece of brass wire about a foot long, turned with a pair of pliers to form an eye in the middle to attach the line, and an eye in each end to fasten the snells. Spreaders that have a swivel in the middle of the wire and underneath it an eye, so that three snells may be used, may be found at the shops. The bait is the small white grub most easily found in dead and partly rotten second-growth pine trees or logs, from which it has to be cut out with an ax. The man who catches perch for market does not trouble himself to provide more than two or three grubs, for as soon as he catches one fish, he has two baits, using the eyes after the fish is dead, for bait. When the spreader is thrown through the holes cut in the ice there is nothing to do but to wait for a bite. If a perch takes one bite the matter is settled—it is only necessary

34

to rebait and lower the hooks, for each time without fail there will be a fish brought up for each hook baited.

But it is through the hot dog days that the perch fills a really void spot in angling. It is then a host of people of both sexes, young and old, leave the city for rest and holiday; for them perch fishing in lake or river is a pleasant recreation. It is always better fishing in swift-running water—all kinds of fish bite sharper than in more quiet streams—the reason of course being that their food is whirled rapidly by them, and unless they seize it hurriedly, they miss it altogether; therefore when perch are on the shallows, at the beginning of the season, lying usually between waving masses of weeds, it is a good plan to drop the line in at every likely spot, leave it there only a few seconds, and almost immediately the perch, if feeding, and provided it is not alarmed by the approach of the angler, will dash at the bait and take it. Perch, like all other voracious feeders, are easily scared, at least mature fish—usually all kinds of small and young fish are not so easily frightened.

When perch are caught in stagnant ponds or muddy lakes, before cooking them it is well to take the skin off; by so doing the wooden, muddy taste is avoided. If fried without the skin they make a very delicious and palatable dish. When fish are caught in running water or cool, spring-fed lakes there is no need to take their skin off, it is only necessary to scale them well, their flesh being white and sweet. So that either for game or edible purposes, when possible, choose a running stream to fish in.

THE CHAIN PICKEREL

THE chain pickerel is known under various names; in the South it is called jack; in some parts of the North it is the federation pike, but to most people it is known as the eastern pickerel. It grows to a length of two feet and weighs occasionally eight pounds, though the average is much smaller.

The pickerel is the most numerous of all the Esox family, which includes the great northern pike and the muskellunge. All are voracious, marauding tyrants, and do not assemble in schools, but prefer to live to wage war alone.

It prefers dark and sluggish water, old roots, tree trunks that are decayed and muddy bottoms are its delight. Whenever introduced into new waters, by its rapid increase and voracious habits, it will soon exterminate or drive away all other vari-

37

eties of superior game fishes, the perch and sunfish excepted. These are only safe because they are protected by their sharp spines, which can be erected at will to defend themselves.

The pickerel loves to lie in summer, on warm days, among the lily pads and weeds, generally near the shore; there he stays quiet as a stone with his long nose just peeping out, watching for his prey. Their growth is rapid, and their ravenous disposition causes them to be favorites with many anglers, since they bite vigorously at almost any bait of live fish or spoon, and boldly resent capture in a manner which only strong tackle can withstand.

While feeding he has two places of vantage, one is in from eight to ten feet of water where the bottom curves up sharply toward the bank. Here he lies close to the bottom, and strikes in at any small fish that passes near the shore; the other place is in the weeds, out of which he springs like lightning, keeping his jaws closed tightly

38

until within a few inches of his prey, then opening them wide and shutting them together with a violent snap. He immediately returns with the capture to his haunt, and then works it around from the cross way he always strikes, and swallows it head foremost. Their jaws are mere skin and bone, the skin often easily tears, and the bone forms no substance in which the hook can be embedded, so that if the hook does not slip off it is frequently broken off. Nothing but wire or gimp snells will stand for a moment the terrible teeth of this ferocious fish, of which he has several rows as sharp as needles and mostly pointed inward.

Pickerel are always on the watch for food; for that reason fishing with live minnows or trolling with a spoon is the best method of capturing them. Sometimes they are caught in still fishing also by skittering, but perhaps the most effective way is trolling, as it gives the most natural imitation of a small fish swimming. When trolling in deep water, just outside the lily pads, the boat should be rowed so that the spoon runs about two feet from the surface, a small-sized spoon being the best, and it should not be allowed to sink over a foot deep. When fishing in shallow water near the weeds, the young angler should be careful that the spoon spins or revolves properly, and the boat keeps on the move, or the spoon in that case will sink. If the hook catches a weed, reel in the line to remove from the hook any grass or weeds, as the fish will not touch a spoon unless it is perfectly clear of weeds. Let out thirty or forty feet of line. The rod should be short and stiff, the reel a good one that runs easily. If the angler can manage it, with the help of a good rower, two rods may be used, one on each side of the boat, one spoon of copper, the other of steel. In that case, if the fish strikes one of them the other rod should be taken up by the rower and reeled in, so that the angler can attend to the fish without any hindrance. The boat should be rowed with a slow, steady motion without splashing or sudden jerks. If possible, be provided with spoons made of copper, brass and steel. Sometimes pickerel will take a brass spoon when the sky is clear, and when cloudy prefer a silver or steel one. There is no advantage in having a spoon painted red on one side, it is best to have both sides showing the metal, for the spoon is intended to imitate the minnows swimming.

It often happens that good-sized perch take the spoon, if so they should be played in the same manner as the pickerel. When the fish strikes, it is like a double pull, don't be too quick to hook him, nine times out of ten he will hook himself; a sudden jerk often pulls the hook from him, a quick turn of the wrist is all that is required to fasten the bait, should it hold the fish will struggle, and perhaps rush some distance away. If he goes toward the weeds the reel should be held firm and the fish leisurely guided

41

away; then slowly reel in. At times he will make a struggle, at other times he will come quietly till he gets to the boat and then suddenly dash off; in such cases be prepared to let him work and give him the line he wants. After he is brought back to the boat get the net ready, for in taking a pickerel from the water more fish get away than are taken—a net saves such disasters. When the fish is laid in the boat have a care how it is handled; place the foot on its head to keep it still while extracting the spoon from its jaws; this done, give the fish a few sharp raps on the head with a short stick or piece of iron, to stop it from leaping out of the boat; a pickerel often makes a harder fight in the boat than in the water.

In still fishing with live bait either from a boat landing or anchored out among the weeds, a longer rod is more convenient. Use the same line and reel as for trolling, but a float should be attached, and the hook best suited is a 2|0 or 3|0 needle-eyed Sproat hook, fastened on a piano-wire snell, with a swivel at the upper end; a few lead shots as sinkers are fastened two feet above the hook to keep the bait below. The float should be adjusted according to the depth of water and the minnow should swim about three feet from the bottom. The best bait are minnows, or small chubs or shiners, with the hook put through the upper and lower lips, near the tip of the nose; a minnow hooked so will be lively and swim for some time, till the pickerel or perch takes it.

The boat should be moved if no strikes are made and another spot tried. When the fish takes the minnow let him run a short distance, he has only got it in his mouth sideways and will stop to kill and swallow it; when he starts away again, then is the time to strike sharply, and he will be hooked. Keep him from the weeds and let him run till he is tired. This is always wise, if the fish is a good size; hurried angling always leads to disaster—but never let the line be slack, as a tight line stops him from unhooking himself. When he is brought near the boat the same method is used in landing as in trolling.

Skittering is a favorite method of the country people, but this requires some practice and considerable skill; young anglers should not attempt it, because the rod used is sixteen or eighteen feet long, heavy and stiff; some use a spoon, others fish entirely with minnows and young frogs, or a piece of the white part of a perch shaped like a fish, and a piece of pork rind is often very successful—about twenty feet of line is the limit to the cast required. If in the boat, throw the bait toward the shore and bring it back along on the top of the water in little jerks—two casts will decide the luck, if nothing rewards move on to the next clear opening of the water and try again. When the fish strikes, hold him steady and then slowly move him to the boat and land him in the usual way.

Fishing through the ice for pickerel is

The Chain Pickerel

a favorite winter sport if the ice is free from snow. A dozen or more holes are cut through the ice in a circle over the feeding grounds where they lie in summer, only in deeper water—a fire may be built in the center, and tie-ups are baited and placed on the holes. These tie-ups are made of a piece of thin wood three feet long and three inches wide, a few inches from one end a hole is bored, through which is thrust a round stick like a section of a broom handle, and long enough to extend well across the hole in the ice—a short line four feet long, with a hook and leaded sinker is tied to the short end of the thin board through a small hole bored for the purpose. The hook is baited with a minnow, then placed in the water, the thin board is laid down on its edge with the short end at the middle of the hole in the ice and the round stick straddling it. When a fish pulls on the line at the short end of the board, it will raise the long end, thus indicating the looked-for event. On the long end of the lever a signal flag is fixed, so that the angler goes from one to the other as the flags go up; all that is to be done is to take the fish out and rebait the hooks. The fish need only to be laid on the ice, where they soon get frozen stiff, and it has been stated that these same fish if kept frozen through the winter will, in the spring on being placed in warm water, come back to life and be as lively as ever.

Opinion differs as to the edible qualities of the pickerel, but if cooked properly, when fresh and the scales taken off, their flesh is white, flaky and sweet, especially when caught in clear spring water. They are caught in great quantities in the Great Lakes and are sold in the market at a fair price. When pickerel are taken from swift running rivers, they improve greatly both in gameness and edibility. Even in swift water their habit is the same—they choose a quiet lair, then pounce in the rapids for their prey, and with it return.

THE SUNFISH

THE little " sunny " is enshrined in the hearts of old boy anglers as well as young boys, as their first love. All the best qualities of fish rolled into one, except that of size; it is one of the hardiest and prettiest species of the finny tribe. North and South, wherever clear water is to be found, this little favorite is ready at all times to gratify the eager angler. In Southern States it is known as the bream or brim; in other localities as the sunfish, pondfish, tobacco box and pumpkin seed, which it is supposed to resemble, but the most popular is the boys' endearing term, " sunny." Dr. Brown Goode says: " The pumpkin seed and the perch are the first trophies of the boy angler. Many are the memories of truant days, dreamed away by pond or brookside with twine, pole and pin hook, and the slow homeward trudge,

47

doubtful what his reception would be at home. Pole gone, line broken, hooks lost, the only remnant of the morning's glory a score of lean sun-dried perches and sunnies, and mayhap a few eels and catfish ignominiously strung through the gills upon a willow withe.

The sunfish grows to a length of eight inches and a weight of half a pound. In coloration it rivals the gayly tinted fishes of the coral reefs in tropical seas. The predominating colors are yellow and blue, dark blue-gray on the back, shading to a lighter tint of greenish brown; the belly a bright orange, and the face is streaked in yellow and blue, with long ear flaps in black. It is well armed with a fierce array of spines, and shows a temper, especially after nest building, unusual in small-sized fishes. Consequently they thrive and multiply almost beyond belief in ponds and streams too small for bass and too warm for trout. It prefers clear and still water, living in and about weeds and grasses. In the spring

Pickerel

Sunfish

Perch

of the year the female prepares herself a circular nest by removing all grass and other dead aquatic plants from a chosen spot of a foot in diameter, so as to leave bare the clear gravel or sand; she then digs into the sand about four inches and deposits her spawn, which she watches and cares for like a hen does her chicks, till the small fish appear. All fish, even those of her own species, that intrude on her privacy, she will drive from her nursery, and attacks shiners, minnows and killies, often killing them in defense of her home. Sunfish are gamey and eager biters, and earthworms are their delight; they will also readily rise to a very small artificial fly with a vim and dash much in the manner of the black bass, their bold and larger cousins. Like the perch, any old tackle will catch them at times, but if proper angling outfit is used to capture them, larger fish and more gamey play is the result. If a boy has a light rod, or better still, a regular eight-foot bamboo, not too pliable or yet too stiff, such a rod covers the wants of all fresh-water bottom-feeding fish, but the sunny needs a finer line than the perch. It also needs much smaller hooks, of size from 8 to 10, and the float should be small, for it takes it with such a snap, running away at a clipping pace, that young anglers would lose half their pleasure fishing for sunnies without a float; the patience is not wearied by waiting for it to bob, they keep it bobbing all the time. Adjust the float so that the bait hangs a foot from the bottom. This is done by using a sinker to find the depth of the water. Place two or three No. 8 split shots about six inches apart from the snell, to sink the bait. Angle worms or earthworms are the most successful bait. They should be small of size—those of a reddish-pink color are the best; put only one worm on the hook, and be very careful to loop it over the hook, leaving a small end to wriggle in the water. No kind of fish are more eager to take a bunch of worms, and no larger fish are attracted by an indescribable bunch, which must appear to the fish a curious and unusual sight. Every time a fish is caught, the old worm as well as all broken parts should be removed, and a new one, live and kicking, should take its place.

In fishing for sunnies there is little or no necessity to move to a new place if the fish stop biting for a while; at such times throw a few worms in the water to attract them to the bait, as sunfish shoal together in large numbers. Sometimes the whole morning can be spent in one spot, constantly landing fish where the bait is placed, as there seems to be some system whereby the fish get to know food is to be had, and they come from all around that part of the lake or stream. Throw the bait in gently without much splash, little time elapses and not much waiting before the bob goes down and another trophy is brought from the water; fifty sunfish is by no means a great morning's catch. If the amateur is able to cast a fly much better sport can be enjoyed.

Most anglers while trout fishing in hot weather with line and leaders of extra fineness are bothered with many little sunnies that too often take the fly intended for larger game. The extra outfit necessary is simply a very fine three-foot leader, the smallest of flies—two are sufficient—one at the end, the other eighteen inches away. Of course in fly fishing, no float should be used, as the flies are simply cast on the surface of the water, and the fish dart up from below and seize them.

In casting it requires some little practice at first to force the flies any distance, but if the novice lets out but twenty feet of line he will manage it better than if he tries a longer cast. The best flies are the black gnat, gray and brown palmers, and the coachman, but any flies will do for sunnies if they are of the smallest size possible. The object of fishing with a fly is to imitate the natural fly which is constantly seen dropping on the surface of the water, then floating down a few feet and rising again in

the air. If fishing on clear still water the
flies should be cast out as far as possible
from the angler, then the tip of the rod
gradually raised to draw the cast slowly
back in little jerks. This should be repeated
till the fish takes the fly; when that occurs,
immediately give a gentle twist of the wrist,
which hooks him. He will at once make a
short run near the surface of the water,
and then take a dive below. Give him free
play until he tires, then bring him to the
boat or shore. As the sunny has a particularly hard, bony mouth, he may not be
hooked firm, often being held only by a
thin skin, so that it will be safer if a small
hand net be provided, and used by the left
hand; it should be placed in the water below
the fish, which can be gently led into the
net after the line is reeled in short.

In fishing a stream of running water,
cast the fly down a runway, and let it go
into quiet water, for sunfish choose to lie
in still places. Wherever the force of
the water takes the fly it will turn off and

circle round the sunnies' hiding place. In such runways a worm is just as effective; indeed more so, because nature is imitated exactly. Another good fishing ground for sunnies is near the shore of large lakes. Row the boat and anchor it so that it rests on a bed of lily pads or near tall rushes, using a short line and float with worms for bait; throw in the line where there are open spaces. The float assists to keep the line from getting entangled. The angler will be kept busy with the scores of sunnies and perch, all fighting to get the bait first. The best time for fishing is from sunset to dark, this time being when all surface-feeding fish are on the lookout for food, very different from catfish and eels, whose food is entirely obtained at the bottom, and at any time of the day, though both are partly nocturnal feeders. While rowing round any large pond or lake of clear water the young angler should be on the lookout for the nest of the sunfish, which lies invariably in very shallow water a foot or two deep, and from the boatside can easily be seen in the light, sandy places. But they are only occupied in the early spring; in summertime it is deserted by the old as well as young fish. A nice string of a dozen sunfish, weighing half a pound each, makes a very pleasing and agreeable dish if properly fried; they are better eating than the perch, but not so sweet and flaky as the bass. There is no question but that the little sunny is a popular idol with all who angle for him. I have seen whole families together—father, mother, daughter and son sitting contentedly, each with more or less improvised rods, passing the summer days with infinite pleasure, now and then a shout of glee proclaiming another prize has been boated. The pleasures of the summer visitor on mountain lake are certainly incomplete unless some member of the family brings home for the table a dish of sunnies to be fried.

THE CARP

THE carp is a native of Asia, and was introduced in America in 1831; its acclimation has been wonderfully successful, especially in the South, where it continues to grow throughout the year and sometimes attains a remarkable size. It is a favorite of thousands of modest fresh-water anglers whose pleasure lies in quiet, peaceful delight in the midst of restful scenery of the woods and meadows. The carp is a handsome fish, with scales of a golden bronze, which are large in size. There are numerous species of this family. The mirror, or king carp is named on account of the few and extraordinarily large scales, which run along the sides of the body in three or four rows, the rest of the body being bare.

The leather carp, which has on its back either only a few scales, or none at all, possesses a thick soft skin which feels velvety to the touch. Then there is the golden carp, popular in small fountain ponds and household aquariums. But the common carp has become very abundant in certain lakes and rivers; those found in the latter are much the best to angle for, and are of better flavor. In lakes it prefers a muddy bottom, particularly near the roots of water lilies; in the rivers it likes those parts where the stream is slow and stagnant, with the bottom thick in mud, as it lives principally on vegetable food, much preferring the seeds of water lilies, wild rice and water oats. In captivity it will eat lettuce, cabbage, soaked barley, wheat, rice, corn, insects and their larvæ, worms and meats of various kinds. They can readily be caught with dough, grains of barley or wheat, worms, maggots, wasp larvæ and sometimes pieces of meat and fish. The carp is very tenacious of life, more so than any other fresh-water fish, with the exception of the catfish and eel. In Holland they have a way of keeping them alive suspended in nets and feeding them with bread and milk. To insure the best sport when angling for carp, it requires great preparation and care. The line should be entirely of medium-sized or fine round gut, clouded gut preferred, and a very light porcupine quill float, with one good-sized shot about six inches from the hook, which should be a No. 5 or No. 6, and baited with a red worm. If possible the depth of the water should be taken the night before the angler intends to fish; this can be done with a sinker, and a quantity of ground bait, composed of bread kneaded into little balls, should be thrown in the place. Arrange the distance between the float and the shot so that the latter may exactly rest on the bottom, weighing down the float to about " half cock " and letting the gut below the shot and the bait lie on the ground. Early in the morning and occasionally late in the evening are much the best time for carp fishing, and the all-important thing is to take especial care and keep out of sight, as the carp is very shy. A forked stick can be put in the bank for the rod to rest on while the angler moves back out of sight. Approach the water cautiously and drop the bait exactly in the spot you have plumbed the night before, and again leave the bank a few steps, lying down on the grass, taking care still to see the float. When there is a touch give time, even until the float begins to move off, then strike and, as the carp has a tough mouth, there is little chance of losing him. The angler will find that catching a carp with rod and line is always a difficult and uncertain operation, especially if the fish is a large one; they are very wary and patient, sometimes swimming round the bait for a long time before they touch it. Young carp of two pounds or less are much the best to take the bait, and it constantly happens with the best anglers that large carp will not be taken with this or any other mode of fishing; but if they are to be caught at all it is thus: Some anglers prepare for their sport by " ground bait-ing " with a thousand or more angle worms twenty-four hours before they expect to fish, and while fishing throw worms into the water. There is no fear of over-feeding, as their appetite is unlimited. The carp is now pretty well distributed all over the United States. Between 1877 and 1885 the streams of very nearly the whole Pacific Coast were stocked, and the free distribu-tion of young fry by the United States Bureau of Fisheries led a great many per-sons to apply for them and plant them in ponds, from which they afterward found their way into streams that contained fish much their superior. The carp is now rap-idly coming into demand as a market fish. From the Illinois River alone, over six million pounds are taken annually. New York City consumes over seven million pounds yearly.

They are taken in very large numbers from the big lakes—Erie, Chautauqua, On-

The Carp

tario, and from those waters are fairly good eating; but if taken from small stagnant ponds they are both tough and are of a peculiar muddy taste. When hooked they resist and pull pretty hard, but make no fight. Their excessive shyness makes angling for them much more interesting sport than would otherwise be if such were not the case.

DACE OR FALLFISH

THIS bright silvery little fish is very abundant, and delights in rapid, rocky portions of large streams and in the deeper channels of clear running brooks. It is one of the largest of the minnow family, reaching a length of eighteen inches and about two pounds in weight. It is extremely common in the Delaware River and its tributaries, moderately abundant in the Susquehanna. Both in shape and movement it is not unlike the brook trout, with which it lives in amiable relations, although it will live in water of a much higher temperature than the trout; still, it prefers cold and rapid streams. Like other common and familiar fishes it is called by many names in different localities, some of which are silver chub, cousin trout, roach, the corporal, and many others. When half grown it is netted and used extensively as bait, being hardy, bright and silvery in color. Trout anglers have no liking for it, because it constantly rises and takes the fly intended for more desirable fish. In smaller rivers like the Beaverkill, it is so numerous that twenty dace will rise to one trout; but they often rise short, getting just pricked in the lips, so that they are very often whipped off in recasting the fly. They invariably lie at the rocky bottoms of swift running water, feeding on vegetable matter, worms and insects, constantly rising to the surface for any floating food passing above. I have caught them up to two pounds' weight on every possible bait. They will take a small artificial or live mouse, a silver minnow, hellgramite or small frog, but for general all round fishing they give more play on the artificial fly or live worm. In running water the regular trout tackle is best suited to dace fishing, a light nine-foot rod, oiled silk line, with a six-foot leader and small, easy running click reel. For worm fishing the hooks should be No. 9 to

No. 11. No leaded sinkers or float are necessary, dace being always on the lookout for passing food. The running water carries the bait along the surface, and at times takes it down below; but wherever it goes, if within reasonable distance, the fish on seeing it darts quickly above or below, and takes it with surprising quickness. The mouth of the dace is not large like those of the perch, eel or catfish, so that at times it misses making the hook, but often manages to take the worm. On being hooked it fights desperately for a time, running back and forth in rapid succession; sometimes, though rarely, it will rise above the surface.

When a fish is hooked that measures over twelve inches long he should be gently led to the shore and played over the pebbles or sand from out of the water, if a net is not handy; do not attempt to lift a dace bodily from the water, he will surely get off the hook, and so get away. A small hand net is indispensable. It is possible to lift smaller fish from the water to be unhooked and then basketed. They are so plentiful and bite so vigorously that the basket is easily filled, and in place of trout they make, so far as game is concerned, a very fair substitute. There is no special place where they stay; in deep pools or

Chub and Dace.

bright shallows, both are equally good, and they will take the bait readily at all times in the day and season. They are equally voracious with the artificial fly, so long as it be small in size; all flies are alike to them, though the black gnat seems to be a never failing lure. The regulation brook

65

trout outfit of a six-foot leader, and three flies tied a foot and a half apart will be suitable, but the flies should be of the smallest size. It matters not where the cast is made; in the center of the stream or at the sides, dace will dart for it, not always, to be sure, getting hooked, for they very often rise short, go for the upper fly, miss it, but take the second or first, and so get hooked. Their resistance is similar to that in taking the worm: a desperate and hard fight for a short time, and then suddenly give out, unless they succeed in getting off, which they do many times. In extra swift water their play is exactly that of the brook trout. I had quite a large one playing some time this last season, and was quite sure of its being a trout, till it gave a leap from the water nearly two feet high. Much to my surprise I found it to be an unusually gamey dace. This was in rapid water, rocky bottom. In pond or lake, fishing for dace with worms, exactly the same tackle and methods should be used as in fishing for sunfish; they inhabit the same localities and are usually called shiners or silver sides, but in such situations of quiet water their actions are not nearly so gamey in resisting capture, nor do they grow so large a size if the same water contains the ravenous pike or bass. Most of the larger sized fish, when they venture out to deep water, are caught and devoured, so that it is in brooks or rivers that dace fishing is at its best. Another species, called the redfin or golden shiner, which never attains a length of over ten inches, is often caught both on the worm and fly. They are very numerous in clear cool lakes, and are often found in great schools at the mouth of small rivers and brooks. Hundreds of them can be taken in a short time on the worm and flies, if the hooks are not too large. The chub is a very leathery mouthed and hardy fish; he is coarser and more bony, but very handsome in form and color. Much stouter tackle is necessary when angling for chub than for the dace.

Bait Angling for Common Fishes

There is so much similarity between a small chub and a large dace that it may be as well here to point the most distinguishing feature of each. In the first place the mouth of the chub is much wider and the scales are larger than the dace, and the color is also darker, though in some waters where the dace grow large in size their color becomes quite dark on the back, losing the silvery hue. The difference between it and the chub is so slight as to render it extremely difficult sometimes for the young angler to determine whether he has caught the former or the latter—chub in some waters grow to the weight of five or six pounds. On bright days a fly is the best method of catching this fish, and good sport may be had from an anchored boat, by throwing a fly just under the bushes, which overhang the banks of the stream, it being characteristic of this fish to lie under trees and bushes, waiting for insects which drop from them. A good method of angling for chub is to hook a live grasshopper through the shoulders; if carefully done it will live for some time. Use a No. 8 or No. 9 hook, and affixed to a piece of gut about three feet long. Throw the bait under the bushes and draw it gradually through the water; it should have a single shot to sink the bait. Chub are extremely shy, and the angler should keep out of sight as much as possible; and he must be approached with great caution. Chub will also take worms and small minnows, for such bait the angler can either fish with a float or without; but the leader should be strong, with one or two shots to sink the bait, which should be dropped into a deep hole or under a bank, let sink to the bottom, then gradually raised, moving along with the current. When a chub is hooked give him plenty of line, for he shoots very violently away for a few seconds, but soon gives up the fight. The chub is not held in any great esteem as a food for the table, its flesh being coarse and hard.

PIKE PERCH OR WALL-EYE

THE wall-eyed pike as an angler's trophy may be placed between the perch and the pickerel; for all round fishing it hardly reaches the pickerel in gameness, though to some it is superior. It is essentially a bottom fish, and the bait it goes for best is minnows, lob-worms and occasionally rises to the fly. Owing to its nocturnal habits the best time to angle for it is from sunset to dark; in fact, it is fished for after dark by many people on moonlight nights or by the aid of a bright lantern. The wall-eye is known by many names, for it is abundant all over the continent, and is still being regularly distributed as a desirable fish both for its game and edible qualities. In various localities it is known as the glass-eyed pike, blue pike, yellow pike, salmon and jack salmon. In Canada it is called the doré, where it

Wall-Eyed Pike.

grows, to a weight of twelve pounds. In shape and coloration it is similar to the perch, but has a larger mouth and very sharp teeth. Its eyes are also very large and glassy, being more prominent than most fish, well fitting it for seeking its prey by night. The wall-eye is found in all depths of water, but prefers to be near the bottom, either of rock or of gravel, in clear as well as cold water. It loves to lie in the deep pools at the foot of ripples or where

71

the current is strong and deep, near small dams and under sunken logs, or shelving rocks and banks, often near the timbers of bridges in deep water. It will only enter shallow water in lakes and streams in search of food or at spawning time. It feeds on every kind of small fish and does not even spare its own offspring. Insects, larvæ, crawfish, and worms are devoured in great numbers, and even young frogs and small snakes are sometimes preyed upon. Its usual weight is from two to four pounds, but it grows to fifteen pounds under favorable conditions. Its flesh is highly prized as a food fish, being white, firm and flaky, and is of an excellent flavor, which makes it a commercial fish of much importance, especially on Lake Erie, from whence it is shipped in large numbers to the city markets, where it always commands a ready sale, being in great demand during the Lenten season. There are three ways to fish for the wall-eye: on lakes it should be fished for in comparatively deep water, over pebbly bottoms, with a live minnow or crawfish, particularly minnows with silver sides, such as the dace, roach or redfin. In rapid currents, pieces of fish with the skin white or silvery, and trimmed in a shape so that it will spin nicely. I have caught them on a spinner with a bright colored bass fly on the end. But certainly the best sport is with the fly at evening on running streams. The most likely places are casting over deep and swift water, just at the foot of rapids, or on a rocky lee shore, when there is a brisk wind blowing. In such places they congregate in search of minnows that are rendered almost helpless by the churning water. I consider the pike perch, especially in running water, a good gamey fish, he takes the bait quite savagely, and when hooked is a vigorous fighter, pulling in jerks and tugs, which are strong and powerful. For that reason very young anglers should not attempt to fish for pike perch unless a grown-up is in the boat or by the river-side. For lake fishing the rod should be stout and well built, with a strong silk or fine cuttyhunk line; the hooks should be snelled with gimp or piano wire, because, like the pickerel, their sharp teeth easily cut through the stoutest gut. Have a sinker dropped down to find the proper depth to adjust the float, three or four shots should be placed on the snell to keep the minnow down in deep water. Some anglers use two hooks, but I do not see the advantage of it, except the extra excitement of landing a double, which is sometimes very inconvenient and often leads to serious loss of tackle as well as patience. Certainly more fish are caught on dull, cloudy, windy days, and in the evenings. In minnow fishing quite a large hook is advisable—size Nos. 2|0 to 3|0, if the fish run a good size. The method of hooking a minnow is the same as for pickerel—that is, place the point through the under lip, coming out of the upper lip near the tip of the nose. When a wall-eye takes the bait he makes no rushes or runs with the line, but swims leisurely away, sometimes taking the float along the surface of the water without going under; let him go some distance; after a while, if he does not stop, raise the tip of the rod quickly, and it will hook him. If he does stop after moving a short distance, then strike good and hard. A strike should be merely a quick, sharp move of the wrist only—not the arm, for that is likely to wrench out the bait from his mouth; the wrist movement is just right to impale the barb. After being hooked he will tug violently for a time and keep up the game all the time till he is reeled in. He never makes any effort to take runs; even up to the time he is landed he just simply pulls and tugs. The larger and heavier fish often dive to the bottom after being reeled nearly in, and when at the bottom there they stay, jiggering, and it takes some strength to move them, especially on a light rod, which requires most careful work. I have never been successful in getting a wall-eye to rise to the fly on sunny days in lake fishing—it is only in the late evening, and then not often. They will rise to the fly much more readily in white foamy water below a dam or falls, though this fish is most uncertain to locate, being much given to roaming about in search of food. In fishing the rapids let the fly be allowed to wander at will, either on the surface or under, just as the current takes it, even giving line that it may go some distance away around rocks and along eddies, for the fish lies mostly at the bottom. When the fly passes over it, it rises with a quick dart, especially if the fly has sunk two or three feet by the force of the water. One fly is sufficient placed at the end of a four or six-foot leader, similar to that used for bass. As to the size of fly, it should be what would be called a large trout fly or a small bass fly. In color use a dark fly in the morning, dark gray hackle, black hackle, gray drake; for the evening use a white miller, silver doctor or coachman. Of the three the latter is the best. As soon as the

Minnows

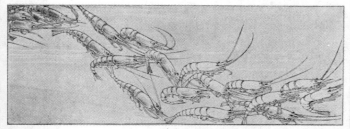

Shrimps

Good Live Bait

fish takes the fly, a tight and firm hold on the rod should be kept all the time, for, while not so long a fighter as the bass, the wall-eye is every bit as strong, and while it lasts, in swift water, a ten-pound fish is indeed no mean work for a tyro to tackle. And I warn any young amateur angler he must have already gained a calm and steady demeanor, and also should have had some practice, both on the large perch and pickerel before he tries a hand on the fly in rough water for the bold and handsome wall-eye. If he does manage it successfully his power is sufficient to try his hand at the gamey bass. I was once wading a rocky and turbulent stream, hooking a fish that immediately shot out of the water. Not knowing what it was, after playing some time another fish took a fly, and both leaped quite near enough for me to see I had on a bass and wall-eye. Though I landed both after infinite patience by dragging them up the pebbly beach, they gave me such a peculiar fight as I have rarely experienced.

It seemed strange they never tried to dart
away in opposite directions; if that had
been attempted it would have been the last
of the business. They evidently decided to
work in unison to their own destruction.
Dr. Brown Goode states " there is no better
pike perch fishing in the world than that
which may be had in the vicinity of Lake
City, Minnesota, in Lake Pepin and the
adjacent waters." The tackle in use there
is a three-jointed bamboo rod, twelve
feet long, a click reel placed on the
front of the hand and on top of the rod,
with thirty or forty yards of braided silk
line, and a Sproat bent hook—No. 3|0
tied to a single length of twisted double
gut or gimp.

The pike perch is common all over Europe, and is known as the Zanda; it is
angled for in much the same way as for
pike. In Germany it is sold alive, being
kept in tubs in the markets. Millions of
pounds of this fish are caught in Russia
and Sweden, where it is salted and a kind

of caviare is made of its roe. The wall-eye is quite common in most of the rivers and lakes in New York, New Jersey and Pennsylvania, where it seems to thrive well wherever it is placed.

BOTTOM FISHING FOR BROOK TROUT

THOUGH we cannot class the speckled beauty among the bottom feeders, yet there are times and places when he cannot be caught otherwise. This is usually in ponds and lakes which have been artificially stocked, especially if the water has been dammed but a short time; in that case their food is almost exclusively taken from the bottom. Only at rare intervals, mostly at sundown, do they rise to a fly. Trout are always on the lookout for feed; if not on the surface for flies they are certain to be nosing for worms, grubs, insects of all kinds that live in the water, mostly on the bottom.

In some ponds brook trout are fed artificially—that is, on chopped meat or liver; in that case the fish lose nearly all their game and fighting qualities, for the obvious reason that there is no need to fight for their food. In swift water they are forever on the alert, and dash after their food with great rapidity; but the trout caught in still fishing on the bottom rarely resist capture more than other bottom fish not classed as game. In fishing such lakes, large or small, the most important thing is to find the proper depth with a sinker, and when found, adjust the float so that the bait lies exactly six inches from the bottom. If a catfish is hooked move away to another spot, for where catfish abound they fiercely attack the trout with their spines to stop the trout from taking the worm. The trout has no armored spines to defend himself with, and his only safety is in flight. But should the catfish continue to take the bait adjust the float so that the bait lies a foot higher from the bottom; by that means the catfish will be less liable to interfere. Brook trout, if of a good size, will more readily seize a young live minnow than a worm, but the latter is no mean bait, especially in the early spring. For trout, worms should be scoured; the method of scouring or toughening worms is described in the chapter devoted to them. The worm should be most carefully hooked on through the skin only, not through the

Trout.

body, for of all fish the trout seizes the bait with wide open mouth, and swallows the hook instantly; there is no nibbling or even smelling, but a wild sudden dash, and down it goes.

It is a common practice with country fishermen to use a method called "chumming" in still water for trout, which is sim-

ply nothing more than a plentiful supply
of worms chopped up and at times thrown
over the boat side after it has been anchored for a while and all is quiet. This
attracts the trout to where the bait is placed,
and they very soon take it. There is little
of the true sportsman in this method of
angling, but the result of it often succeeds
in taking a large number of fish which
otherwise would not be caught. I have
often tried every possible means to lure
them up with the fly, but failed to get a
rise during the daytime. At evening, when
flies are more numerous on the wing, the
trout will rise for fifteen or twenty minutes,
then suddenly stop and again drop to the
bottom; but in that short time half a dozen
brace are caught on the fly, no matter what
size or kind. They are after flies, and they
tackle all that appear on the surface.

On such a pool I took a friend who was
very anxious to land some fish. We
whipped our flies till thoroughly tired,
when I suggested that we try worms. I

knew there were plenty of fish, and as time was limited we did not wish to return home with empty creels. After securing sufficient worms and finding the right depth, we at once began to land fish, and in half an hour took twelve brace of sixteen-inch trout, which just filled our creels with the nicest and most even size of fish I had caught that summer. But the sport was tame; a single run and a few minor struggles was all there was in it. No sooner had the bait touched the bottom than a trout was hooked, and all were taken in one place, without moving the boat from its anchorage. In bottom fishing for trout the tackle need not necessarily be over fine, a three-foot leader with good sharp Sproat hooks, three or four split shot for sinkers and a light float. The rod is better if short and somewhat stiff, the usual bait rod being about the right article.

As to the location where they lie, it seems they most often move about in schools, so that in fishing one part of the pool with poor results, it is best to move to other quarters. They usually lie fifteen feet from shore, unless in the middle there are shallows with sunken logs or roots of trees; here they get food of all kinds of insects. In such a place, when one is caught others will usually follow. On very warm days they will seek the deeper, cooler water, leaving it for the shallows when the sun goes down, when they rise to the fly. It is little or no use fishing very early in the morning; they are more likely to bite after the sun is up till early morn; then again just before sundown to dark is by far the best time of the day. This is likewise true of most fish, either game or coarse. Exactly the same conditions apply to deep pools of running rivers, where the larger trout hide; brown trout grow big and gross in such deep places. There they make their lair, driving all from the place but the larger fish; here they are often seduced by a worm if properly played. The best way to do it is to fish for them by letting the current take the worm where it wills, allowing it to run round and round by the force of the water till the fish strikes, but the worm should be hooked by the skin, kicking and wriggling as it goes, just as it would if driven naturally by the water. Should the fish be a very large one, it is best to let out plenty of line, though at all times kept taut. When the first rush is over slowly reel in and work him gradually on to the shore, making no attempt to stop the rushes he may feel inclined to indulge in. Patience is the watchword in handling a large fish from the bottom. Neither the brown or brook trout is likely to give much of a fight when caught under these conditions, for the water is usually slow moving if deep, and his habits have become suited to the water. The same species caught behind a bowlder in swift water at once leaps into the air, running up stream at a clipping pace, and if the tackle is extra fine some careful work is necessary. In deep pools trout often get behind rocks or sunken logs to get off the hook; in such cases the position of the angler should be moved, holding a tight line all the time.

It is necessary to have one or two small split shot on the leader to keep the worm down below, otherwise the bait by the force of the water floats on the surface.

SALT-WATER BAIT

A GREAT many salt-water anglers consider any old bait will do for sea fishing, but this is not entirely true; sometimes there are fish which will certainly take everything put before them in any shape or manner. But watch the veteran, how careful he is, how little he talks, while he cuts up his bait or arranges his killies and shrimps on the hooks. Examine his catch at the end of the day, and compare it with that of the man who chucks things around. Without any doubt shrimps and bloodworms stand first on the list as the best all-round bait for sea fishing; next comes live killies for the larger fish, and pieces of clam for the smaller. But the different shell fish are in many cases splendid lures—shedder crab, hermit crab and fiddlers. Then comes strips of dead fish—herring, mossbunker, porgy, sea robin,

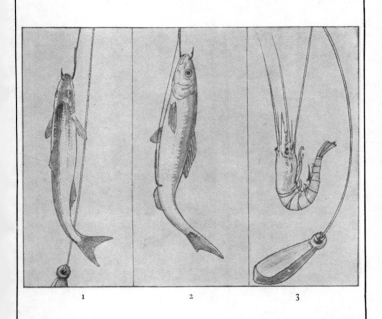

1. Single hooked live minnow
2. Double hooked live minnow
3. Single hooked shrimp

Proper Method of Hooking Live Bait

spearing. In emergencies, when bait is short, parts of the fish caught are put to use for bait. The most important part of the outfit is to have a first-class bait can and box easy to open and shut, as well as secure, so that the bait may not escape. Such a thing gives the angler great comfort as nothing is so annoying as to find the bait die or escape before angling begins.

To purchase bait for sea fishing that is sufficient for a day's sport is quite expensive in some cases, and fortunate indeed is the angler who can catch the bait himself on his way to the fishing grounds. To get shrimps a stout net is required, and the time to get them is at falling or low tide. They are to be caught in many of the small pools in creeks and inland bays. When netting them the net should be moved swiftly through the water as near the bottom as possible and dragged through the weeds and seagrass. If two anglers are together, a couple of thousand are soon scooped in, one netting, the other picking out the shrimp after they are dumped on the dry land. They should at once be placed in the bait box and covered over with a supply of cabbage weed, a thin green sea plant that is plentiful where they are caught.

If the box is not trailed in the water during the time the angler is going to the fishing ground, the shrimps should be kept cool and the water repeatedly changed, so that they are about the temperature of sea water. In this manner they can be kept alive. They will live some time in the water after being hooked. After they are dead they turn a white color, and in that state are of no service.

To get blood or sandworms, the necessary tool is a strong spade, which can be hidden among the grass after use for future occasions. Bloodworms are not so plentiful or so easy to get as shrimps. They are partial to a strong, muddy sand, and are dug up about six inches from the surface. The best places to find them is in sandy, dark, muddy places, where mussels and small shell fish cling to the edges of the water.

After being dug out they should at once be placed in the box with cabbage weed, without water or sand, but, like shrimp, must be kept cool or they soon die, and therefore become worthless because they turn white and have an unpleasant odor. The box should be dipped frequently in the water to keep the weed moist; if the weed is allowed to dry it shrivels up and the worms quickly die.

Live killies are caught in much the same places as shrimps, indeed many are caught in the net with them. They are hardy little fellows, and will keep for a long time in water that is changed and kept cool.

Of the crabs the fiddler is most abundant and easiest of capture, though the angler must be thin and spry to get at them, for they are astonishingly quick in running to cover. Fat anglers are no good in catching fiddlers. The shedder crab is the hardest of all crabs to get, that is the reason why they are the most expensive to buy. All crabs are better if kept alive; they will lie quiet in a cool dark place if covered over with plenty of seagrass.

Heat is sure death to all creatures whose habitat is salt water. It is strange so many anglers forget this one point of temperature for bait. They will row for miles exposing the bait to the blazing sun, and when ready to fish find their bait all shriveled up and partly cooked.

Finally, regarding chum, any kind of fish chopped fine is useful, but menhaden is the most effective, the same may be said of chopped shrimps.

It is a wise plan where two or three anglers go together, for one who thoroughly understands bait, to devote his whole attention, while the others angle, to preparing and hooking on the bait for the others, and at intervals assist in landing the fish if needs be. If one is unwilling to do this the day through, then divide the time so that all can have a share in the actual sport.

PLAICE OR FLUKE

NO sea fish is so popular or so well known as this; it is called by a variety of names, which are often confounded with other species. In some localities it is called plaice, summer flounder or turbot flounder; whereas the flounder is known as the flatfish, winter flounder, muddab and nigger fish. The two can be more easily distinguished by the plaice having a large mouth and the flounder a very small one. Next to the halibut the plaice is the most important and valuable flatfish on the Eastern coast, they average in size from two to eight pounds, though specimens have been caught up to twenty-five pounds. Like others of its species, the plaice habitually lie upon the bottom, where their peculiar shape and color protect them from observation and also gives them an excellent opportunity to capture their prey. It is next to impossible to distinguish them from the sandy bottom when they are lying still. They are found mostly in the bays and bayous where the bottom is muddy and grassy, but it is not unusual to find them in the shoal water along the sandy beaches of the coast and bays. Very shoal water seems to be particularly attractive, and they are often found at the water's edge, embedded in the sand, with only their eyes in view. When alarmed or in the pursuit of their prey their movements are very swift, and the quickness with which they bury themselves in the sand is quite wonderful. Plaice may be taken from the early part of June till September and October; in Florida they are taken throughout the year, but are most plentiful in the summer months. In Jacksonville they are commonly taken in company with bream, black bass and other fresh-water fish in winter as well as in summer. They feed on small fish, shrimps, crabs, squid, and are frequently seen at the surface of the water rapidly swimming and even jumping out of the water in pursuit of sand eels and sand smelts, and will also feed on dead fish thrown out from the fish houses. Favorite fishing grounds are on sandy bottoms at a depth of eight or ten fathoms, or in a channel, near the sides, either from a boat at anchor or one that drifts slowly along with the tide. The method is to fish with one hook six inches from the bottom and another hook two feet above, tied on a strong three-foot leader; use a sinker just heavy enough to hold to the bottom, and live killies for bait, though herring, spearing and mossbunker are considered just as good as killies; if no live bait is available, small strips of snapper or porgy cut in the shape of a fish will often be a taking bait.

A well known practical angler says: " The usual method of hooking live killies is by the lips, so that they will swim naturally, but the majority of Jamaica Bay fishermen put a killie on the hook by inserting the point of the hook into the back of the killie near the dorsal fin and then pass it along under the skin toward the tail as far as the bend of the hook will permit, then again push it through the skin to clear the barb."

Drifting is the method of fishing for plaice that is productive of the best results, but good messes are sometimes caught while fishing at anchor, as the boat is drifting with the tide the angler is fishing practically in stagnant water; that is, there is no friction from a current on the line or bait, therefore the killie on the hook can swim about as if entirely free, and even if hooked in the back will not kink or double up, as is the case in still fishing. When the baited rig is out and is being trailed along, its distance from the boat should be at least six times that of the depth of water where fishing, so that a plaice when hooked can display his resistance of capture to better advantage. When still fishing for plaice, a killie if impaled on the hook through the lips, appears more attractive than if hooked through the skin of the back, because of the action of the tide, but the chances for capture is not so good when a plaice strikes, for sometimes it will strike short, especially when the killie is more than three inches long. The most successful rig for local waters is a leader from three to four feet in length, fastened a few inches above the sinker, and a 5|o Kirby-Limerick hook tied to the end of the leader, and another a foot from it. In drifting or trolling the long eel grass and sea weed will collect on the line, leaving the bait on and near the end of the long leader clear. In using these long leaders do not allow the lead to go to the bottom too fast, because the leader will go down parallel with the line and become entangled. Use heavy sinkers according to the thickness of the line.

Plaice do not always put up a fierce fight, but will usually show enough resistance in capture to please anybody. When he takes the bait the strike should be followed up with a gentle jerk of sufficient force to embed the hook firmly and to rouse the fish into action. If he is from ten to fifteen pounds it is no child's play to land him; sometimes he will shake like a bulldog, then come up like a lamb, only at the last moment to give such a sudden kick as to easily rack the nerves of old hands. On such occasions the only thing to do is to keep a tight line, stop reeling in and wait till his tantrums are over, for without a net, when he has a kicking fit on, he is liable to make short work of the tackle while he is being lifted from the water. Many a good sized fish is lost at the edge of the boat. To be cock-sure often means a slip, for one of those sudden plunges gives him his freedom. The advantages of fishing for plaice and flatfish is this, they can be fished for at any time of the day or night; no waiting for tides or certain kinds of weather; they are hungry all the time, and always willing to take what is offered to them.

Plaice or Fluke

In " Food and Game Fishes of New York," Doctor Bean states : " This fish frequently ascends fresh water streams. It moves off in winter into deep water, then comes back in summer near the shores. The plaice is sometimes seen feeding about wharves whose supports furnish it a suitable hiding place from which to dart on small fish when they are congregated in schools. I have seen large individuals cautiously wriggling their way upward in the concealment of a wharf pile till within easy reach of a school of silversides, when a sudden dart into the midst of the school would result in the capture of a fish, and the plaice would leisurely sink to digest its victim and prepare for another onslaught." It is their habit to constantly shift their position, probably in search of food, so that good results one day may not be the same the next in the same spot. They have a rugged and powerful mode of resistance, especially the larger fish, which often succeed in getting off the hook or breaking the tackle, for they fight all the way till taken from the water.

If cooked when fresh, they are extremely good eating, the flesh being white, juicy and of good flavor.

THE FLOUNDER OR FLATFISH

Next in importance to the plaice is the flounder, sometimes called the winter flounder and also the flatfish; it is much more abundant and does not grow to so large a size as the plaice. The flounder is a cold-weather fish, biting from February to the beginning of May, and again from October to December. They are always on the bottom, feeding upon shells, young crabs or whatever they can find among the stones and in the mud. They prefer soft, black mud bottoms, and the boat should be anchored half-way between the middle of the channel and the edges. At high tide they scatter well over the flats; at low tide they gather together in the center of channels. Their mouths are very small, and as they would be unable to seize and kill other fish, they never come to the surface in search of their prey, as do the large-mouthed plaice.

They are more permanent residents of the localities which they inhabit than any other fish on our coast, for both in winter and summer they appear to be equally abundant.

If the angler does not succeed in getting bites it often happens the fish lie buried in mud, so that if the bottom is raked with the anchor or with the oar it will often stir them up to take the bait, and if the sinker is a heavy one, and gets embedded, move it around to stir up the bottom. The hooks should be small and placed within a few inches of the sinker. The best bait are sandworms, clams and mussels.

There is very little sport in landing flounders, because they rarely attain a weight of over two pounds, but they make up in numbers what they lack in weight, and the angler more often than not, fills his basket with this toothsome little fish, and if fried when fresh they are equal to any salt-water fish in sweetness and nutriment. All anglers have a tender regard for this little favorite, perhaps because he is the first fish to make his appearance in the spring, almost while the ice is in the bays. The angler, before the long winter is past, is eager to again stir him up from his hole in the sand bars with a clam rake. But toward the middle of May his big brother, the plaice, puts in an appearance and remains with us till the frost comes again to nip our fingers. Angling for flatfish is a favorite pastime of women and children. The fish lie in water not too deep, and from the boat may be seen diligently biting at the bottom. This makes it doubly interesting, for they are remarkably agile—after being hooked they skip off, but are suddenly reminded that they are wanted above. The rod is of little service in flounder fishing—hand lines are invariably the rule; just a simple line, snelled hook and sinker. No leader is required. Two or three hooks may be attached if the fish are plentiful, and it is not uncommon for three fish to be hauled in at once.

All the hooks should, however, be as near the bottom as possible, for that reason a small wire spreader can be attached, whereby the three hooks can be tied all of even length from the wire—about six inches, the same distance as the sinker. The flounder is so numerous that they may be caught anywhere if the bottom is suited to their habits. Like the plaice, they are ever ready to bite at all times during the day or night, and wind and tide play no part in the success of their capture.

THE CODFISH AND TOM COD

THIS well known and prolific fish is not esteemed by anglers for its gamey qualities, but solely for its value as a table food. It grows to a considerable size, and is usually found together in great numbers and is readily captured. It is a deep water fish, caught mostly in the open sea in from eight to forty fathoms of water, from the fishing bank boats and sailing vessels. At nights during the summer months they sometimes run in close toward the shore, where they may be caught off the long piers at Coney Island and other places.

They move in schools periodically to and from the shore, according to the seasonable change in temperature. The codfish, as well as the tom cod, is a winter fish when so many species that supply food are absent either in the deeper water or have moved southward in warmer waters. The codfish begin to bite early in October, and so continue through the winter till the end of April.

They feed upon all marine animals that are smaller than themselves, which are found in the same water with them; anything that is digestible is greedily taken by this voracious fish. In searching the bottom for shells and worms they often pick up objects which can hardly be regarded as nutritious. It has been noted at various times that the codfish has had remarkable objects taken from its stomach, such as finger rings, fragments of oil clothing, and the heel of a boot has suggested the idea that large codfish sometimes swallow the fisherman. So greedy are they that they have been caught with their stomachs filled to the greatest possible extent, having fish in their mouths which they have been unable to swallow for want of room, and in this condition they were still biting at the hook. Is it any wonder that they rapidly grow to an enormous size, frequently over one hundred pounds. A lady while on a fishing excursion on board a yacht caught a cod which weighed one hundred and thirty pounds, though the aver-

Cod and Tom Cod.

age market fish is from six to twelve pounds. In later years they are not caught as large or as plentifully as they used to be.

In fishing for cod nothing is needed but stout lines and heavy sinkers and special cod hooks, which should be placed as near the sinker as possible. It is entirely a matter of choice with the angler how many hooks are used, though the limit seems to be three.

The same may also be said regarding the choice of bait used in cod fishing—clams, crabs, worms or killies, it is all the same to this ravenous fish, who, after taking it, makes no resistance whatever, and the ease of its capture is but limited to its weight.

It has become quite a saying. " He bites like a codfish, " anglers will exclaim when a fish of any kind gives no fight. So that this fish is perhaps the least desirable to catch from the angler's standpoint of gamey sport; not so, however, is it despised, for it is a valuable prize, if a big one, and the proud angler goes home with the assurance of at least two good meals for his family. If the cod is cooked within a few hours of its capture the flesh is much harder and tastes sweeter than those fish purchased in the market, that have probably been caught three or four days.

The tom cod in form is a miniature of

the codfish, rarely exceeding ten or twelve inches in length. In some places it is called the frost fish, owing to the fact that it becomes more abundant in the early part of the winter, when it approaches the shore and even ascends the rivers and creeks for the purpose of spawning; and although most abundant near the shores and in the streams in early winter, they are found along the coast at all seasons of the year. Angling for them begins in September, and the North River piers are lined with people of all ages who enjoy catching this dainty little fish. They are bold biters, playing fairly well when hooked. To get the best play and sport use a small springy rod five to seven feet long, a light line and small reel, with a light three-foot leader, to which may be tied three hooks. As the tom cod are exclusively bottom feeders the hooks should be close to the sinker, which must be heavy enough to hold on to the bottom. Sandworms are by far the best bait, though shrimps or clams may be used.

Bait Angling for Common Fishes

The tom cod can always be found near piers and bridges in the rivers and inlets during the winter months. As a food fish they are esteemed in many localities as a great delicacy. They are not caught in vast numbers, like most of the smaller sea fish, such as the porgy, but they are a favorite with most anglers because they resist capture a great deal more than their giant relative and namesake.

SEA BASS

THIS fish has an enormous appetite and is well known in having the reputation of being the most determined and persistent biter of any fish that swims the sea. Though sluggish in habits, its large and powerful fins are able to propel it through the water with great swiftness. During the breeding season the male fish develops a large hump on his shoulders, which takes away the fine graceful appearance which distinguishes the female. When they are first taken from the water their color is remarkably beautiful, a dark blue, purple and olive being the predominant colors. They have a large and powerful mouth (which is characteristic of the bass family), and will take a generous bit of almost anything that is eatable. It spends its time continually nosing about the loose stones and in the cavities among the rocks that have seaweed growing upon them. In this they get various crabs, fishes and other creatures. Upon such feeding grounds the sea bass congregate in great herds, rooting and delving among the holes for such delicacies in water from twenty to fifty feet deep. They are a bottom loving and bottom feeding fish, and rarely come up to the surface. The temperature of the body is low, being very nearly that of the surrounding water, and their digestion is slow. Though eager feeders, their rate of growth is not rapid. They retreat in all probability into water of greater depth, where they pass the winter in a somewhat torpid state. The best time to catch them is during their feeding time, which is usually during the lull of the waters between the turn of the tides. The largest fish are caught on the fishing banks, where steamers during the greater part of the year make daily trips to the Cholera Banks off Sandy Hook and

Sea Bass

Long Branch. These steamers are well patronized by thousands of practical anglers who seldom fail to bring back trophies weighing four to eight pounds. The bass caught in the bays, estuaries and back waters are much smaller, weighing but half to one and a half pounds. These fish rarely, if ever, go up into brackish water. The best places to angle for them is in deep channels, holes under sedgy banks and over wrecks or on a bottom where the black mussel is found, this being a favorite haunt where many may be captured. They will take the bait from Decoration Day to October, but the larger sized fish are taken in inside waters from September to October. Like the fresh-water bass, he will sometimes break water, but not till he is drawn near to the boat and ready to be netted, when he will suddenly make a vicious leap, shaking his solid body in all sorts of wriggling and muscular contortions; from the moment the hook gets into his leathery jaws he makes a sturdy fight and dies hard. It frequently occurs that when a fish is hooked and being hauled in, several others follow along almost to the surface of the water, then the hooked fish makes his final effort to escape by leaping above the surface. At such times it is absolutely necessary to keep a taut line; if hooked at all, and the hook is strong, he is sure to be landed, if reasonable care is used.

Almost any bait is suitable for sea bass —skimmer clams, mossbunkers, shedder crabs, generous pieces of clam, live killies, sandworms, shrimps, herring, squid and cut menhaden—all of these will be taken with avidity; one is as good as another, for the

Sea Bass.

sea bass is always on the feed, always hungry. Greater success is achieved on bright, sunny days, when the wind makes a slight ripple on the water. The tackle used should be a good stout rod, multiplying reel and a strong line of generous length. Leaders are only necessary when fishing for the big yellow autumn bass, which are very shy and wary. Late in the season use the No. 2 Sproat hook or a No. 2 Carlisle. A heavy sinker is required to hold firmly on the bottom, and the hooks should be tied quite close to the sinker. Some use only one hook, others use two, each having on a different bait. If baiting with shrimps place two or three together on the same hook, for this fish is one of the few that go for the largest bait, and as his mouth is so ample he is sure to be well hooked with a big bait. Between the turn of the tide the angler is sure to be busy for the short time it lasts. The feeding grounds extend along the coast from Delaware to Maine, wherever the seaweed grows from beds of mussels. It is eminently a coast fish, seldom venturing far above the bays and back waters.

As a food fish the meat of the sea bass is excellent; it is white, the flakes are solid and compact, not so soft and watery as the cod, but more succulent and delicate in taste; it is best boiled, but epicures regard it as superior in a chowder. As a food as well as game fish it may be placed next in rank to its cousin the striped bass, which of course is not classed among the bottom feeders.

TAUTOG OR BLACKFISH

THE tautog is one of the species of parrot fishes, stockily built, hard scales and harder mouth; it has a long row of spines running nearly the whole length of its back. The color is of a greenish-black, sometimes bluish-black, with metallic reflections and having irregular bands of a deeper hue. He is as slippery as an eel, and salt-water anglers like to fish for him because he is a strong and hard fighter. For that reason he is not a fish young people should try to handle unless well able to take care of themselves. Although not a large fish, only averaging two to three pounds, individuals weighing ten and even fourteen pounds are by no means unusual. The largest tautog on record was obtained near New York and preserved in the National Museum. It weighed twenty-two and one-half pounds. The tautog is found in greater or lesser abundance from St. Johns, N. B., to Charleston, S. C., and is known in various places as black-fish, tautog chub, moll, will-george and oyster fish. East of New York it is usually called tautog, a name given it by the Narragansett Indians. The tautog do not like very cold water, and take refuge from it by returning in winter to somewhat deeper water than that preferred in summer. Here they appear to take shelter under the stones and crevices of the rocks, where they enter upon an actual state of hibernation, ceasing to feed, and their vital functions partially suspended. It is certain that they do not retreat far from the shore in winter, and that very cold weather, especially in connection with a run of low tides, often causes very remarkable fatalities. As may be inferred from its haunts and from the character of its strong, sharp teeth, the tautog's food consists of hard-shelled mollusks, squids, scallops, barnacles

118

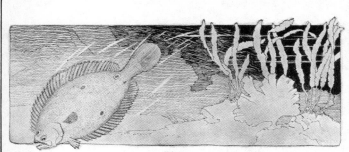

Plaice

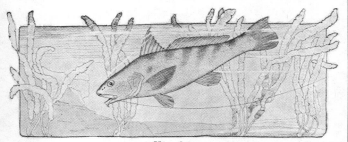

Kingfish

Blackfish

and sand dollars. Many of the mollusks they swallow, shells and all, ejecting the hard parts after the flesh has been digested. Angling from rocks for tautog is a favorite pursuit of amateur fishermen all along the coast, particularly about New York, where there are precipitous shores, the fisherman standing.

On Long Island Sound and other protected waters, they are usually fished for from boats anchored among the reefs or near wrecked vessels, and shell-covered piles and wharfs and rocky bottoms are very good places. At some places they bite best upon the flood tide; in others they are voracious during the ebb tide. Thunder accompanying a shower is an indication that no more of them can be caught. The appearance of a porpoise infalliby puts an end to the sport. Dull weather, with an easterly wind, is generally the omen of ill luck. Some anglers bait for them by throwing overboard broken clams or crabs to induce them to renew their visit. When the cold of winter benumbs him the tautog refuses to eat any more, and not until the return of the warm spring does he begin to regain his appetite. It is in April and May we have the best angling, and though they frequent local waters all through the summer, not many are caught in the warm months, until fishing begins again in October and November. The regulation bait in spring is the clam—preferably soft-shell clam—for at this time many anglers say the tautog has a tender mouth. In the fall both crabs and lobsters, as well as fiddlers and rock crabs, are the favorite baits, and sometimes they will take sandworms and shrimps. Large numbers of tautog are caught by the anglers who go out daily on the fishing steamers in the open sea. All, or nearly all, use the regulation saltwater tackle—a short stout and heavy rod, strong line and large wooden reel. Such tackle is necessary for outside fishing, and the hooks should be very strong, but not large in size.

Tautog or Blackfish

For inside fishing lighter tackle will do, though the hooks should be the same. In baiting the hook with a small crab it should be done so that the point of the hook passes through from the belly to the back, taking great care not to crush the body in hooking. If the hook is put through nearer the head it will last much longer. A shrimp should be hooked in the same manner by placing the point underneath near the tail, afterward drawing the shrimp over; in that manner it will live for some time. The sinker should be a heavy one, and the two hooks tied about six inches apart as near the sinker as possible. No leader is required, but the gut snells must be very strong to withstand the sharp teeth when he is tugging at the bottom. The tautog feeds entirely on the bottom, where shell fish abound. He rarely if ever interferes with the smaller fish that swim near him. When fishing inside waters arrange so that the boat can be anchored near the edge of the tide, close to a rapid current, where the reefs or rocks are about twenty to thirty feet deep.

The tautog is provided with a pair of strong crushers situated in the back part of its mouth and consisting of two flat groups of ball-shaped teeth between which they crush small shell fish before swallowing them. When it takes the bait it passes it on to the crushers, when a peculiar succession of bites is felt by the angler, who loses many a fine fish by being too hasty to hook him. After the first indication is felt of a fish taking the bait it should be struck sharply, but not too soon, for the angler can feel a second and even a third tug before the strike is given, as he bites with a strong will, but when he is fast he gives such a bulldog fight, along with hard pulls, which only strong and well-made tackle can withstand, especially when he is of a fair size. The tautog bites much like a sheepshead, but with less power. You feel the premonition, but when he dashes aside the pull is weaker than the sheepshead. This refers to a tide-running fish of from three to eight pounds, and which feeds on the edge of the swift water. He has a white nose, and is fair game. The tautog, which feeds close to the base of the rocks, is an adept at getting hooks or sinkers fastened in the clefts, for so soon as he bites and feels the barb he darts under or between the rocks, leaving the angler thankful if the fish will liberate the hook or sinker as the price of freedom.

PORGY

THIS is another plentiful and common sea fish known by many names. In New England it is generally called "scup," while about New York it is paugy or porgy—both being abbreviated from the Narragansett Indian name, scuppaug. On the Virginia coast it is called the "fair maid." The porgy is found along our coasts at all seasons of the year, but it is more numerous in June and July. The first run takes place about the beginning of May, and consists of large breeding fish weighing from two to four pounds, measuring up to eighteen inches in length. On first coming near the shores they do not take the hook readily, being too much occupied in spawning, and two weeks elapse before they can be caught on the hook. They present themselves in large schools of immense extent, numbering many millions,

moving very slowly at about the rate of
three miles an hour. Yet in some years
they appear only in small numbers. The
porgy is mostly a bottom fish, and depends
very much upon mollusks and shell fish for
subsistence, its especial food being small
crabs, shell fish, shrimps and small minnows, but for bait the clam is by far the
best, they also like the claws and legs of
shedder crabs, each leg when split open will
make two or three baits just the right size
for this fish. Generally they take the bait
eagerly, following it up from the bottom,
biting after a quick short run with a sharp
nip. They will also go for small sandworms and bloodworms when they will not
touch other bait. They are gamey and
plucky little fish; if fine tackle is used
they will give play for their size as
good as the fresh-water perch. Sometimes the larger fish just nibble, and
the angler will hardly feel a bite, yet
the hook will be stripped clean. For
that reason small hooks are much the

best for porgy fishing, and they should always be kept as sharp as a needle. No. 5 to No. 7 are the size hooks, the larger size should only be used when the big fish are running. Although porgies are mostly bottom feeders, they often do at times swim half-way up to the surface; in such instances they follow the bait as it goes to the bottom, then go for it when still. The sinker should be heavy, to keep the bait in one place; a light sinker is driven by the force of the tide, sometimes a distance up from the bottom. Place the first hook six inches

Lafayette and Porgy.

126

above the sinker, the second hook another six inches above, and it may be of a larger size than the lower hook. Some anglers use three hooks to entice those fish swimming above the bottom. The bait must be small, only just large enough to cover the hook; in that case even the smallest nip will catch him. The porgy has a large head and hard mouth, so that when even a touch is felt on the line give a sharp quick strike to firmly embed the hook. They seem to bite much better on bright, sunny days, when the wind gently ripples the water, and the first part of the flood tide is always best to strike a good school.

For tackle use a light springy rod, and though a reel is unnecessary, it is sometimes convenient to give out longer line at varying depths. Use a very fine line, with hooks small, strong and extra sharp. From the first of August to the last of October many anglers enjoy catching this gamey little fish; outside the sport of landing them they are much coveted as a pan-fish.

In flavor the porgy is surpassed by few other fish on the coast, although its super-abundance causes it to be undervalued, the smaller ones especially being sweet and nutritious. Of their abundance in former times almost incredible accounts are given; they swarmed to such a degree that their capture ceased to be a matter of sport. When the line was thrown overboard it could be immediately withdrawn with the assurance of having a fish on both hooks. Any number of fishermen from boats could take five hundred to one thousand pounds of fish a day without the slightest difficulty, the limit of the catch being simply the ability to find a sale.

But now such numbers are rare, yet from one to two hundred is not an uncommon day's catch. The younger fish are devoured in immense numbers by blue fish, halibut, cod, shark and other ground feeders. Yet this seems to make little difference to the enormous shoals that appear at times during the summer months.

LAFAYETTE OR SPOT

THE name Lafayette was given it by the New York fishermen in consequence of its reappearance in large numbers in that region having been coincident with the arrival of Lafayette in this country in 1824. It had been known before that time, but only in scattering numbers. Dr. Tarleton Bean says that the name spot is derived from the presence of a dark blotch about as big as the eye near the root of the pectoral fin.

Other names of this species are, goody, old wife, roach and chub. The spot swarms on the Eastern coast during the hot months of July and August, and is caught as late as September. It is a small fish, rarely exceeding ten inches in length or a pound in weight; but for its size it is game to the last, and puts up a fight to shame much larger fish. It is one of the best pan fishes caught in the sea. In both these qualities it much resembles the porgy, though as a fighter it is much superior. It ascends small streams into rather brackish water, and is a common associate of the white perch. Immediately the lafayettes are running it is a signal for hundreds of men, women and boys to crowd the North River piers so thick that on some occasions there is little elbow room for comfort. These people are there not so much for excitement, but to furnish their friends and families with a mess of fish that is much enjoyed. And when these fish come in with the new flood tide in large numbers, as it often does, catches of a hundred or more are not remarkable. Such, however, are not all of large size; some fishermen put back all but a few of the large ones, fishing just for the sport of catching them, but most all carry big and little ones home at nightfall with great pride. They may also be caught in great numbers at Rockaway, on the Jersey shore,

Cape May, Atlantic City and as far down as Mayport in Florida. The most successful bait are small pieces of clam or small-sized sandworms. At certain times they are erratic and will take only shrimp or the leg of shedder crab, so that the angler will do well to supply himself with a small variety of bait. They will even change biting from clams to shrimps between forenoon and evening, then change their mind at night and want some other bait. All bottom-feeders are good biters at night, and the lafayette is no exception to this rule. They take the hook with a sly, tentative nibble, sometimes hardly felt by the angler; but on feeling the barb away they go, darting off, back and forth with remarkably bold breaks. So quick are their movements that they are frequently hooked on the back or the tail. Their actions are very similar to the brook trout, in the rapid darts up and down, as well as back and forth. The main point in catching lafayettes is to have small, very sharp hooks, attached to a leader about six inches from the sinker, which should be just heavy enough to hold on the bottom. In such places as the docks and piers the tide does not affect the water, and a small sinker is enough, but where the tide runs heavy the sinker can be changed. It is easy to feel if the sinker holds well, as the line does not belly out and travel away, but stays in the spot it is placed. As the fish swim near the bottom in great schools four hooks are not too many, and the bait should be fine, small pieces that just cover the barb—a larger bait for so small a fish tempts them to nibble away till they at last take all off the hook without being caught. Hand-lines are more frequently used, but a short, light rod is always more handy and easier to handle a fish of this kind, as it helps materially to land the fish quicker, either fishing from a boat or dock. This little fish does not require a reel, though at times I have seen those huge six or eight-inch wooden reels brought to play on these little fellows often smaller than the reel itself. Some anglers use a heavy sinker and swing it over head fifty feet away, and after getting the line taut, wait for a bite of a fish larger in size.

Even old anglers will not despise a trial at the lafayette, enjoying the sport of these little fish that fight stoutly all the time they are being reeled in. Like the porgy, they are held in high esteem by thousands of anglers who have only good words to say of them. Both these little fish swarm all along the Atlantic Coast in immense numbers, and both bite with the same vim and go. From late in August till the end of September, there is hardly a place where lafayette may not be found, and if the right bait is given them, good sport and, what is more, a good mess, can be caught.

SMELTS

THERE are about a dozen species of
this family, which inhabit the cold
and temperate northern seas, but
they are most plentiful along the coast of
New England and the Middle States. The
Eastern smelt grows occasionally to the
length of a foot, but average about seven
inches, and they appear to associate together in vast schools, somewhat according
to size, so that many fishermen contend that
there are two kinds. But Dr. Bean explains, "that most fish that appear in
schools, mostly all of a size, are the spawn
of a single fish." The smelt remains about
the coast, in the bays, estuaries and lower
parts of rivers throughout the year, save
when it ascends fresh water streams to
breed. As soon as the ice is out and the
water has cleared from the spring freshets,
smelts appear in the brooks, at first in small

numbers, and the run continues till the middle of May. They ascend usually at night, and on the ebb tide, though sometimes there are runs on dark days. During spawning time they will not bite the hook, and seem not to feed much, though at times small creatures, such as young shrimp and killie fish, are found in their stomachs. Smelts have been successfully introduced into many of the large lakes that they are unable to ascend because of dams and other obstructions, but in such waters fishing is done almost entirely through the ice in late winter. They have also been placed as food for large game fish, such as the muskellunge, lake trout, bass and pike. So that to successfully take smelts with rod and line the angler must go in the channels at the mouth of streams, along the edge of small rivers, where they are on the move from salt to fresh water.

From the latter part of August to late December smelts will bite with avidity, and the best time is at flood tide, though

some will bite at ebb tide, and many anglers claim that more and larger fish are
caught at night, especially on dark nights.
The best bait are these mentioned in
the order named—shrimps, bloodworms,
common garden worms and small minnows.
Their favorite bait is shrimp, which should
be placed on the hook tail first, the point

Smelts.

of the hook coming out of the head. The
bloodworm is a long, thick, white worm,
dug up from muddy sand in salt water. It
has a large vein of blood running through
the middle, which should not be pierced,
but it should be hooked through the skin,
so that the blood will not escape. If
hooked in this way it is very tough and lasts
a long time. Minnows are more successful

136

when used at night, as they attract the larger sized fish; they should be hooked through the lips from underneath, with the hook coming out at the top of the nose. The rod should be no longer than eight feet, and rather stiff. No reel is required, the line being tied at the tip, so that when the fish bite it can be lifted right into the boat. Use a six-foot gut leader of medium thickness, and attach to it four hooks, so that the end one will hang one foot from the bottom, the other three hooks being about a foot apart. The hooks should be small and the points sharp. A sinker tied at the end should be heavy enough to hold on the bottom; if the tide runs hard and moves the sinker put on a heavier one. All that is required is that it lies at the bottom and the hooks float well away from the line. When the angler meets with a shoal they begin to bite with such rapidity that they can be pulled into the boat as fast as the bait is put on. There are times, however, when the smelt tries to suck in the bait, especially if it be worm fishing. Many an angler has been perplexed on raising his line to find the hooks stripped clean when he has not felt a nibble. The fish will advance in a leisurely manner, then about an inch from the bait he will stop, opening his mouth very wide, make no effort to touch the bait, but by suction will draw it toward and into its mouth without closing the mouth; that is a favorable time to hook it. Sometimes it rejects the bait after drawing it in, and the bait is often pushed up on the gut snell. But this only happens occasionally, mostly with large sized fish. One of the pleasures of smelt fishing is that they may often be seen in the clear water soon after the bait is overboard, swimming round and fighting who shall get the worm first. They are a swift-moving fish, and when once located a good catch is always the result. If smelts are cooked within a short time after being caught they are most delicious eating; the large fish have an oily taste not so agreeable as the smaller fish. Millions of pounds are sold in the markets, being mostly caught by nets during or just before the spawning season. This practice, if done to most fish, would lead to their rapid extinction, but the smelt is so prolific that one female will contain as many as 300,000 spawn, the greater part of which mature, through the habit of breeding in fresh water.

The method of fishing through the ice is similar to that of fishing for perch and pickerel, the common garden worm being mostly used for that purpose.

THE KINGFISH

THE kingfish is perhaps the gamest of bottom feeders that inhabit salt water. All anglers have the best opinion of him, and with one accord, after he is landed, they exclaim: "What a dandy!" Its gamey qualities, its beauty of color and form, as well as its excellent flavor, caused the loyal citizens of New York in colonial days to call this species the kingfish. In former times, when it was much more abundant in New York Bay, the kingfish and the small striped bass were the crowning glory of old-time anglers. The kingfish is also known as the hake on the coast of New Jersey and Delaware, and as the tom cod on the coast of Connecticut, the barb and the black mullet in Chesapeake, the sea mink in North Carolina, and sometimes also in the South as the whiting. It appears quite early in the

The Kingfish

spring with the weakfish, and is found a good deal in company with it; like that fish, seeming to prefer a light mixture of fresh water, as shown by its keeping in the mouth of rivers, and running farther up during the dry season. It takes the bait quite readily, although not caught in anything like the same number in a given time as the weakfish—thirty or forty at a single tide being considered an excellent catch for one boat. The kingfish run much in schools, and keep on or near a hard, sandy bottom, though they prefer the edge of channels and the vicinity. They bite readily at hard or soft clams or small pieces of fish, and are taken most successfully on the early flood tide. They may be captured about and near oyster beds, especially when the oysters are being taken up, when they may be seen under the boats fighting for the worms and crustaceans dislodged by the operation.

The kingfish is a well-built and shapely fish, high shoulders and small head, with the mouth back under the nose. His mouth, though small, is hard and leathery, so that when he is once hooked he is sure to be fast. However much he fights he rarely gets off. In taking the bait they have a variety of ways in going for it, sometimes just the slightest nibble that is hardly felt. Then at other times they rush at it with the greatest fury, racing off with long runs from right to left, sometimes going at a clipping pace right round the boat, and in this way the gamey fighter keeps it up till he is safely landed in the boat, when the angler will be surprised at the remarkable and determined resistance a fish of but two pounds can and does make.

Though these fish go in schools they are often widely separated. Unlike the weakfish, when a dozen or two may be caught in rapid succession, the kingfish keeps little company with his fellow, and the angler is more likely to land other fish, and weakfish in particular if the bait used is shrimp.

But the difference in the actions in these

two fish are very marked; the weakfish, after two or three short rushes, gives up the game. Not so with the kingfish, he will fight up to the bitter end, making repeated runs all the time he is being drawn in, and a final dash on sight of his captor.

Though I have never seen it, it is said at times to break water, if the line is held taut, playing exactly like the small-mouthed bass, by afterward rushing madly to the bottom, pulling and tugging in angry jerks.

The proper tackle for so bold a fish is a light pliant rod and multiplying reel, a strong light line, measuring at least forty yards, a swivel sinker with a three-foot leader. There should be two hooks, Sproat or Aberdeen preferred, size Nos. 1 to 3. The best bait is shedder crab or sand-worms; also shrimps, bloodworms and clams are effective. In August the kingfish can be caught along the south side of Long Island, off the Jersey coast, at Atlantic City, Long Branch and Barnegat Inlet. Further south they are yet more numerous. In size this fish varies from one to six pounds, the average being two or three pounds. In surf fishing the best time is the first of the flood tide. In this situation, with plenty of room, the kingfish is seen at his best, swiftly swimming long distances, for it possesses great propulsive power, as indicated by its fins, so that a three-pounder at the remote end of the line, with a delicate bass rod, generally induces the novice to believe the strength, speed and endurance of this fish is underestimated.

" Gently but firmly " is the main point in playing a kingfish, for his ways are quite peculiar; though, like the striped bass, he takes the bait nearly always without hesitation. When he does feel the barb he starts away like a shot, accelerates his speed, if that be possible, and, swimming low, near the bottom, after a very long and strong run he stops to jigger and shake. If the angler has never taken a kingfish he will be puzzled with the inveterate persistence in keeping below water and running deep, and

144

the surprise will not be diminished when he finally breaks water fifty to one hundred yards from the rod, if sufficient line is given him; and one will wonder after landing a fish which has taken half an hour to kill that it weighs scarcely three pounds. The vital spark of the kingfish is very brilliant, and he is very tenacious of it, but once landed he exhibits a vanquished look, and his orange-colored eyes and scaly head turn downward as if both ashamed as well as fatigued. But, though the kingfish looks like a deck passenger after a long voyage, the angler is sure of one point in his favor, and the cook, as well as the epicure, will be fully assured of another. Like the striped bass, he is infinitely more juicy and palatable if cooked within a few hours of his capture. He is such good eating that any method employed in cooking is agreeable—broiled, baked or fried. No fish that swims the sea makes a better dish. Certainly no bottom-loving fish plays such a game for the angler's real delight.

CONCERNING THE CRUELTY OF ANGLING

IT is not intended in this chapter to defend anglers against those who assert our favorite pastime is cruel, though most non-anglers do; it is their privilege to be innocent of the true state of things in angling methods. Walton's well known remark on hooking a frog, " as if you loved him," is more to the point I wish to make. The angler's chief attribute should be patience, to tear out a hook bodily from the gullet of a fish is just what Walton wished to be avoided. And it is this practice which is quite common to those using bait who are often guilty of unnecessary cruelty, because most fish swallow, sometimes deep down, the bait taken. It is absolutely impossible to extract the hook from an eel that invariably takes the bait two or three inches down his throat. Most anglers sever the head with a knife, but this is likely to cut the gut.

The most humane and rapid method is to rap the top of the head sharply either on a stone or any hard substance near at hand, so that he is stunned and quiet, then with a knife make an incision from the gills to the mouth. To be sure, this is necessary in nearly all fish that take the worm as a bait, and it is one of the evils of bait fishing against which fly-casters have a true complaint, for many young trout under legal size are caught on the worm and not being skillfully unhooked are of necessity killed, even if returned to the water, for the slightest tear in their gills means a speedy death. Most anglers are loth to spend precious time in properly extracting the hook. Yet it can be done harmlessly by pulling the hook down through the gills and placing it backward to get it out without injury to the fish. In catfishing the case is different, their sharp spines are most dangerous, often poisonous, and the quickest way out of the difficulty is to cut from the gills to the mouth. Catfish are most tenacious of life, such a cut seems to have little or no effect on them. If the same were done to trout it would die immedia-ately. If an eel is skinn̈ed without other injury to it, leaving the head intact, it will live for some time after the operation. I invariably kill my trout at once, with a few raps on the head, before basketing, for two reasons; one that they may not escape, and also it is a nervous strain to have them kicking in the creel while casting the fly; but above all it is more humane to at once kill every fish of any kind, and have done with it. Like other edible creatures, fish are provided mainly for the sustenance of man, after being caught.

Of the many methods of capture, an-gling for them is the most humane. If they escape capture by man they eventually will be eaten either by their own kind or other species.

The pike is no sentimentalist when he

goes for a shiner, or for that matter his own offspring—a fierce rush, in it goes, and all is over till the next follows on, and this continues for all time, the larger swallow the smaller if left to themselves. I have seen a trout tear the limb from a frog in a twinkling, his intention was to take the whole, but a slight miscalculation foiled the feast—only for a minute—then another dash toward the wounded creature, and he too is gone. This same trout (the brown species) being a captive must needs eat, and shortly afterward swallowed four six-inch trout in as many minutes, and would have taken more had he room to place them. Watch a school of young fry madly leaping from the shallows as if trying to escape from their natural element—it is some marauding tyrant taking his daily meal, or perhaps the mother of these young fish, which is an ordinary event in fish life. To eat is the main object of their existence. The bluefish, wanton tiger of the seas, will fill himself full, and disgorge for the mere pleasure of new slaughter of living fish, till the whole surface of the water is a moving mass of wounded and cut-up fish, with a flock of gulls following on to get the fragments. Thus the element of cruelty is no factor; it is not even business, but the survival of the fittest. It would be idle to claim that fish feel no pain, but it is certain that when impaled on the hook, either by the lips or on the roof of the mouth, the pain is not half so annoying as the restraint of their liberty. We repeatedly catch a fish with a hook in his mouth lost by a previous angler. A fish is sure to die quickly, even if lifted harmlessly from the water which gives it life. There is a great difference between drowning a cat and killing a fish by exposure to the air we breathe, the one makes frantic efforts to avoid the choking sensation and struggles to escape, the other calmly and quietly ceases to exist, without pain or perceptible quiver, its jumping being merely an endeavor to get back to water, and naturally pursue the even tenor of its way. Many women and children cannot bear to place a worm on the hook, or even see it done. This, without question, is nothing more than a nervous sensitiveness. I have seen grown children of fourteen (girls of course) scream if they saw a harmless caterpillar, spider or ant. Yet the same children would placidly watch a dog run over. So that the hooking of a worm or unhooking a fish is merely a question of habit, which by practice soon becomes a pleasure——that is, if done for a purpose and not wanton mischief. The famous verse of Byron on the venerable Walton, in which he says that he ought to have a hook in his gullet, depends entirely upon how we look on the question, how the saying fits, as it were. The one spending nearly a century of life, helping others by word, deed and thought, whose every virtue, we read, all men knew; on the other hand, a short, dissipated, selfish life, spreading misery to all who came in contact, even to those who befriended him.

Bait Angling for Common Fishes

Wanton cruelty—to purposely give pain without a reason—all true men abhor, but so small a cruelty as to make unwilling creatures a captive, if for a purpose either pleasure or profit, makes a difference not easily defined. Fox-hunting is a pleasure to the hunter, but a sad pain to the fox, if caught, for the reason of a long drawn out misery, to be at last torn asunder. Fishing is a pleasure to the angler, but no pain to the fish, for he dies a natural death, in place of being torn asunder or swallowed alive by his neighbor. To call it cruel to hook a worm is absurd; fish eat them hooked or unhooked. The only question is that the live bait, minnows or worms, should be handled with proper care, both as to the fish and the bait, with advantage to all.

THE END